English for academic study:

Vocabulary

Course Book

Colin Campbell

University of Reading

Credits

Published by
Garnet Publishing Ltd.
8 Southern Court
South Street
Reading RG1 4QS, UK

First published 2007

ISBN-10: 1 85964 898 3
ISBN-13: 978 1 85964 898 8

British Cataloguing-in-Publication Data
A catalogue record for this book is available from
the British Library.

Production
Project manager: Richard Peacock
Project consultant: Rod Webb
Editorial team: Maggie MacIntyre, Natalie Griffith
Design: Mike Hinks
Photography: Clipart.com; Corbis: Bettmann,
                      CDC/PHIL, Patrick Chauvel, Marianna
                      Day Massey, Laura Dwight, Najlah
                      Feanny, Andrew Fox, Owen Franken,
                      Paul Hardy, So Hing-Keung,
                      Catherine Karnow, Karen Kasmauski,
                      Krista Kennell, Frans Lanting, Danny
                      Lehman, Pawel Libera, P. Manner,
                      Stephanie Maze, Wally McNamee,
                      Gideon Mendel, Sally A. Morgan,
                      NASA/epa, Alain Nogues, Kazuyoshi
                      Nomachi, Tim O'Leary, Parrot Pascal,
                      Smiley N. Pool, Roger Ressmeyer,
                      Reuters, Salvador de Sas, Alan
                      Schein, Katarina Stoltz, Swim Ink 2
                      /LLC, Mike Theiss, TWPhoto, Visuals
                      Unlimited; Getty Images: Scott
                      Barbour, Bart Geerligs, Gilles Tondini.

Excerpt from *Sociology*, by J. Fulcher and J. Scott, (1999)
by permission of Oxford University Press.

Every effort has been made to trace the copyright holders
and we apologize in advance for any unintentional
omission. We will be happy to insert the appropriate
acknowledgements in any subsequent editions.

Printed and bound
in Lebanon by International Press

Contents

Acknowledgements

The Centre for Applied Language Studies would like to thank the many presessional staff and students who have generously contributed to the development of these materials.

I would like to thank colleagues who have commented on these materials and in particular Jonathan Smith and Bruce Howell for their work in proofreading a first pilot edition in 2005.

I would also like to thank John Slaght, Paddy Harben and Anne Pallant for permission to use extracts and sentences from: Slaght J., Harben P., Pallant A., 2006, *English for Academic Study: Reading and Writing Source Book*, Garnet Education.

Colin Campbell, Author, July 2006,
Centre for Applied Language Studies,
University of Reading, UK

Introduction

The aim of this book is:
- to clarify what you need to know in order to use words correctly;
- to introduce over 350 key word families and provide you with extensive practice in their use;
- to clarify the type of information that dictionaries can give you on how to use words appropriately and effectively;
- to provide you with systematic practice in the use of dictionaries.

1. Aims of the book

This book will give you systematic practice in using words that commonly occur in academic texts. On completing the exercises in Units 1 to 10, we hope you will be able to use these words accurately and with confidence in both your writing and speaking.

We hope that when you have finished the exercises in the book you will be able to apply this knowledge, in conjunction with your dictionary skills, to your ongoing vocabulary development.

Although this book is intended for self-study outside formal classes, you should discuss with your teacher any problems you face in using the book. You will find this useful if you do not understand some of the terminology, or if your answers do not match the ones in the answer key.

2. The structure of the book

- **Part 1:** These five units, 1 to 5, provide you with an introduction to vocabulary development, based on words from the General Service List (see below). Each unit focuses on *one* aspect of the effective learning of vocabulary. For example, Unit 2 looks at word classes, i.e., the different grammatical classes that words belong to, *nouns*, *verbs*, etc. Unit 5 looks at word grammar, i.e., how individual words are used in sentences and how they connect with other words, or with other parts of the sentence.

- **Part 2:** These five units, 6 to 10, provide practice in using key academic words, building on the practice in Units 1 to 5. Each unit practises the five aspects of vocabulary learning that were covered in Part 1, starting with multi-meaning words and ending with word grammar.

- **Appendices:** In the appendices there are answer keys to all the exercises. There is also a full list of academic words that are dealt with in Units 6 to 10.

  Also in the **Appendices** you will find an **Achievement test**. This test is made up of sentences taken from Units 6 to 10. You can *either* do this test when you have finished all the exercises in the book, *or* you can do the test twice; once before you start the exercises in the book, and the second time after you have finished the exercises in the book. In this way you will be able to see how much progress you have made in your understanding of words and your knowledge of how words work.

3. The vocabulary in the book

- **General Service List (GSL):** This contains over 2,000 word families that are frequently used in a wide variety of contexts. These are words you will use in both general and academic texts. You may already be familiar with many of these words, but there are many you will be less familiar with or not know at all. In addition, you may not have *all* the information you need in order to use even the familiar words correctly and with confidence.

  In Units 1 to 5, you will practise words from about 150 of the most important GSL word families.

- **Academic Word List (AWL):** This word list contains 560 word families based on words that occur frequently in different academic subjects. They are words that you will need when speaking and writing during your course of academic study. These are not technical words, but ones that you will meet in texts whatever subjects you study.

  The full Academic Word List is divided into ten sublists. The first nine lists contain 60 word families each and the last list contains 30 word families. In this book we introduce word families from the first five sublists. Unit 6 introduces words from AWL, Sublist 1; Unit 7 introduces word families from AWL, Sublist 2 and so on. In total, you will practise words from 300 word families from the AWL.

  You can find the full list on the Internet by entering 'Academic Word List' in any search engine.

● **Technical words:** In addition to learning words from the General Service List and the Academic Word List, you will also need to learn many *technical* words connected with your own subject. These words represent concepts that are perhaps only found in your subject area.

There are a number of ways of learning these words. You can:
- read articles or books connected with your subject;
- listen to lectures or watch programmes connected with your subject;
- find an Internet glossary[1] on your subject.

In all the above cases you should make a record of commonly occurring words and study how they are used. Remember, however, that with some technical words you may not fully understand what they mean until you have been on your academic course for some time.

4. How to use the book

In order to help you use this book effectively, we have included questions below that you may be asking yourself, together with our recommendations.

● *Should I do all the units in the order they appear?*
It is recommended that you work through the units in this book in the order they appear.

● *Should I do all the exercises?*
It is also recommended that you do the exercises in the order they appear within the units and also that you do *all* the exercises. Many words are recycled throughout the exercises, in other words, they appear a number of times in different exercises. Doing all the exercises will give you more practice in recognising and using the words.

● *Is it enough just to do the exercises?*
At the end of each unit, there is an activity which encourages you to *review* all the exercises you have done in the unit, and to write down new phrases or new words that you have learned.

Reviewing vocabulary, i.e., looking again and again at words you have met, is an essential part of learning vocabulary. It is not enough to see words *once* in order to remember them; if you only meet a word once you will not have all the information you need to use it fully and correctly.

It is also useful to record *whole phrases* or *sentences with new words in them* rather than just the words by themselves, as this will help you to be able to use the words when speaking or writing.

● *Do I need a dictionary to do the exercises?*
For some exercises the instructions tell you to use a dictionary, but even in cases where there is no explicit instruction to use a dictionary, a good monolingual[2] dictionary will be of great help to you.

It is important to stress that a good monolingual dictionary will not only be useful in doing the exercises in this book, but will also help you during your continuing language studies.

● *When should I use the answer keys?*
You should check your answers when you finish each exercise. If you have made a mistake, notice the correct answer and go back and look at the exercise again. If you still cannot understand why this is the correct answer, ask one of your teachers.

● *What other vocabulary work do I need to do?*
You will meet many of the words from this book in your other classes as well and this will help you remember them. In your other classes and in your work outside class you will also meet many other words that are not in this book but which are on the General Service List. ***It is important that you keep a vocabulary notebook and make a record of these words and how they are used.***

It is also important that you review the words you learn in a regular and systematic way, for example, by reviewing words at the end of each day, then again at the end of each week and again after two weeks.

---

1   A glossary is a list of words with their meanings. You will find many of these on the Internet if you enter 'glossary + (name of subject)' in a search engine like Google, for example, 'glossary + finance'.

2   A monolingual dictionary is one that uses only one language, i.e., English–English. There are no translations into any other language. In your language studies you will undoubtedly need to use both a monolingual and a bilingual dictionary in your own language.

Part 1: Introduction to Vocabulary Development

In these units we will be studying five aspects of effective vocabulary study based on words from the General Service List.

Each unit will address one aspect, as follows:

- Unit 1: Multi-meaning words
- Unit 2: Word classes – nouns, verbs, adjectives & adverbs
- Unit 3: Word families & word parts
- Unit 4: Collocations
- Unit 5: Word grammar

These five aspects of vocabulary learning will then be used in Part 2 to help you study the frequent word families that are listed in the Academic Word List Sublists 1–5.

Multi-meaning words

This unit will help you:
- learn the different meanings of common words with more than one meaning;
- understand the function of different word classes.

Introduction

One of the problems with using dictionaries to find the meaning of words is that many words have a number of different meanings. If you select the first meaning you find in the dictionary without thinking about the context in which the word appears you may choose the wrong definition and misunderstand the text.

Here are some examples of common words with very different meanings:

Word	Meaning
body	• the physical structure of a person or animal, including the head and limbs
	• a group of people who are connected through their work or a particular purpose, e.g., 'The WHO is an international body concerned with health issues.'
	• a large amount of something, especially something that has been collected, such as knowledge, information and so on. 'There is now a considerable body of evidence to support the theory that life exists in other solar systems.'
capital	• the city where a country has its main seat of government
	• money or property used to start a business

Study tip: Keep clear notes of new words in a separate book as research has shown that good language learners keep organised notes.

Study tip: Note that good learners use context to help them comprehend new words.

Task 1: Choosing meaning from context

1.1 In this exercise you are given three definitions for the bold words in the sentences. Choose the correct meaning of the bold words according to the context in which they appear.

Example:

The government gets a lot of revenue from **duty** on tobacco products.

a) a moral or legal obligation

b) a task you have to do as part of your job

c) a tax you pay on goods you buy

Answer: *c) a tax you pay on goods you buy*

1 The questions can be answered in any **order**.

   a) the arrangement or sequence of a group of things in relation to each other.

   b) a command given by a person in authority

   c) a request for a product to be delivered to you

2 Coursework is taken into consideration in awarding the final grade, so it does **count**.

   a) to calculate the quantity of things or people there are in a group

   b) to be valuable or important

   c) to say numbers in order

3 The **nature** of the task will demand a person with a lot of experience in this particular field.

   a) a combination of qualities or features that define a thing

   b) the physical world, including all living things and features such as the land, the oceans and the weather

   c) the character of a person or animal

4 Fatigue is one of the most **common** causes of road accidents.

   a) frequent

   b) belonging to or used by a group of people

   c) ordinary or usual

5 The whole **point** of this law is to protect the rights of individuals.

   a) an idea or opinion that forms part of an argument or discussion

   b) the aim of or reason for something

   c) a precise moment in time or in the development of something

6 Investing in this company should provide an excellent **return**.

   a) go back to one place from another place

   b) profit on money invested

   c) restarting an activity after not doing it for some time

7 Police arrested 15 people in a security **operation** in the capital.

   a) the process of cutting into a human body for medical purposes

   b) a business, company or organisation

   c) a planned action for a particular purpose

8 There are still numerous one-party **states** around the world.

   a) the condition of a person or thing at a particular time

   b) a country or nation

   c) an area within a country that has its own legal and political powers

9 Young people today have a greater **degree** of independence than 30 years ago.

   a) a unit of temperature

   b) a unit for measuring the size of an angle

   c) a recognition awarded by a university

10 The government plans to **introduce** a system of identity cards.

   a) to bring a plan, product or system into operation for the first time

   b) to tell an audience about a performance or speaker they are going to see or hear

   c) to formally tell people each other's names when they meet for the first time

1.2 Here are ten more words to guess in context. Choose the correct meaning, as in Exercise 1.1.

1 He has strong **views** about the best way to deal with the increase in violent crime.

   a) one's opinions or beliefs about something

   b) what you are able to see from a particular place

   c) a picture or photograph of a place

2 The **terms** of the contract must be acceptable to both sides.

   a) a word or expression used to refer to something

   b) the conditions of an agreement

   c) one of the periods of time that the school or university year is divided into

3 It is difficult to disagree with his **argument** that oil has been the main reason for a number of recent military conflicts.

   a) a dispute between two or more people, usually angry

   b) a set of reasons offered as proof that your opinion is right

4 It is quite **certain** that the continued rise in the temperature of the oceans will lead to catastrophe sooner or later.

   a) confident that something is true

   b) sure to happen

   c) used to talk about a particular person or thing without naming them or describing them exactly

5 There are no simple **solutions** to the problem of global warming.

   a) a way of solving a problem

   b) the correct answer to a problem in mathematics or a puzzle of some kind

   c) a liquid in which a solid or gas has been dissolved

6 A large **number** of conditions can be treated with this drug.

   a) a word or sign that represents a quantity or an amount

   b) a quantity of, e.g., things or people

   c) a single item in a performance, e.g., a piece of music

7 The word "comedy" is used in its broadest **sense** here.

   a) one of the five natural abilities – sight, hearing, feeling, taste and smell

   b) a feeling based on instinct rather than fact

   c) the meaning of a word, phrase or sentence

8 The regulations were introduced in order to safeguard the **interests** of local people.

   a) activities or subjects you enjoy in your spare time

   b) advantages or benefits

   c) amount, usually a percentage, paid for the use of someone's money

9 There is a strong **case** for increasing tax on luxury items.

   a) an example of something happening

   b) a set of reasons why something should happen or be done

   c) a legal matter that will be dealt with in court

10 The patient was in a very bad **way** after the operation.

   a) a method of doing something

   b) condition

   c) a route you take to go somewhere

Language note: A word with two or more unrelated meanings is called a *homonym*.

Task 2: Different word class, different meaning

Words can sometimes belong in different classes. For example, *average* can be a noun, adjective or verb. Some of these words can have a different meaning depending on the word class.

For example, the word *mean* can be a noun, a verb or an adjective, but each one has different meanings.

Word	Meaning
mean (noun)	• an average
mean (verb)	• to have a particular meaning
mean (adjective)	• unwilling to spend money

Study tip: Use a dictionary to clarify the word class of individual words.

2.1 In the sentences below, decide whether the bold words are nouns, verbs or adjectives. Check your answer by looking at the definitions below the sentence.

Example:

The article **addresses** the issue of over-fishing in the North Sea.

a) noun: where someone lives

b) verb: to begin trying to solve a problem

Answer: *verb: to begin trying to solve a problem*

1 Experts believe the current instability in world stock markets will not **last** long.

a) adjective: coming after all the others

b) verb: continue or endure for a particular length of time

2 He was a powerful leader and people would rarely **question** his decisions.

a) noun: a phrase you ask when you want information

b) verb: to express doubts about something

3 The **key** issue in the next election will almost certainly be the economy.

a) adjective: most important

b) noun: a metal instrument used for opening or locking a door

4 Many analysts believe the country is entering a period of **relative** economic instability.

a) noun: a family member

b) adjective: having a particular quality in comparison with something else

5 The company intends to **form** an alliance with a partner company in China.

a) verb: to bring into existence

b) noun: a particular type of something

6 The final decision on the merger will be made by the **board**.

    a) verb: to get on a plane, train, ship, etc.

    b) noun: a group of people who manage a company

7 Environmentalists **object** to the proposed new motorway.

    a) verb: to express disapproval or opposition to something

    b) noun: a physical thing that you can see, hold or touch

8 It is a **matter** of some concern that security at some airports is not up to international standards.

    a) noun: a topic that you discuss, think about or deal with

    b) verb: to be important

9 The company is well-known for its **sound** financial management.

    a) noun: something that you hear

    b) adjective: well-founded, sensible, trustworthy

10 As a result of the bad weather, many flights were **subject** to delay.

    a) noun: an idea or topic of discussion

    b) adjective: affected by or experiencing something

Study tip: When you look up words in a dictionary, note what word class they belong to.

2.2 Use your dictionary to check the meanings of the words in bold in the text below. Write the appropriate definition for the words as they appear in the text.

Education is a pillar of modern **society** and the **subject** of endless, often passionate, arguments about how it can best be improved. In the US, there is **heated** debate following revelations that the country's secondary school students **perform** poorly relative to many Asian and European students. The news coincided with increasing **concern** over the nation's urban and lower-income suburban schools, too many of which are languishing at achievement levels **far** below those of middle-class and upper middle-class suburban schools.

Source: Slaght, J., Harben, P., Pallant, A. (2006). 'The Influence of Class Size on Academic Achievement' in *English for Academic Study: Reading and Writing Source Book*. Reading: Garnet Education.

Word	Meaning
society	• people in general living together in organised groups with rules and traditions governing the way they behave towards one another

a) subject

_____

_____

b) heated

_____

_____

c) perform

_____

_____

d) concern

_____

_____

e) far

_____

_____

Task 3: Review time

3.1 Each of these words from Unit 1 can belong to more than one word class. Complete the table.

Example:

subject	_verb_	_noun_
a) object	_____	_____
b) form	_____	_____
c) key	_____	_____
d) sound	_____	_____
e) matter	_____	_____
f) order	_____	_____
g) relative	_____	_____
h) question	_____	_____
i) board	_____	_____

> **Study tip:** You may need to write down and use a word several times before you remember it.

3.2 Look again at the tasks in this unit and write down any new words or phrases you have learnt. Make sure you record which word class or word classes the words belong to. You may find it useful to write down phrases or sentences in which the words occur.

Word	Word class	Example phrase
duty	noun	customs **duty** on luxury cars

Make your own notes here.

2 Word classes – nouns, verbs, adjectives & adverbs

This unit will help you:
- identify the four main word classes from context;
- expand your vocabulary;
- develop your reading skills at the sentence level.

Introduction

Knowing the word class for an individual word will help you use it correctly in both writing and speaking. The main classes we will look at in this unit are nouns, verbs, adjectives and adverbs.

Educators have a multitude of explanations for why smaller class sizes might be expected to improve academic performance, although frequently the ideas are anecdotal.

Source: Slaght, J., Harben, P., Pallant, A. (2006). Unit 1 – Academic Achievement. *English for Academic Study: Reading and Writing Source Book*. Reading: Garnet Education.

Here are some examples of word classes:

Word class	Words
nouns	educators, multitude, explanations, class, sizes, performance
verbs	have, might, expect, improve, are
adjectives	smaller, academic, anecdotal
adverbs	frequently

Task 1: Identifying word classes in context

Study tip: Sometimes you can only identify word classes from context. For example:
- He **studies** hard for his exams. (v)
- They work hard in their **studies**. (n)

1.1 Read this paragraph and then complete the table after, putting all the bold words in the correct column according to word class. If you are not sure, check the words in your dictionary.

Study after study **ranks** schoolchildren in Japan and other **developed** Asian countries among the best in the world, **particularly** on standardised **tests** of **Mathematics** and Science. **American** high school students, meanwhile, **have slipped** somewhere below those in Greece, Lithuania, Taiwan and Singapore in **advanced** Mathematics and Science. However, **classes** in Asia are **large**; forty students for one teacher would be **normal** in most of the region. In **contrast**, elementary school **class** sizes in the United States **average** about 24, according to the US Department of Education.

Source: Slaght, J., Harben, P., Pallant, A. (2006). The Asian Paradox. *English for Academic Study: Reading and Writing Source Book*. Reading: Garnet Education.

Nouns	Verbs	Adjectives	Adverbs

Task 2: Words belonging to one class only

2.1 Check these words in a dictionary and indicate which word class they belong to.

Word	Word class
growth	noun
entire	
basically	
avoid	
existence	
discover	

Word	Word class
regular	
relatively	
provide	
prevent	
highly	
security	

2.2 Look at the sentences. Decide what word class would fill each gap. Write *v* (verb), *n* (noun), *adj* (adjective) or *adv* (adverb) in the brackets after each gap.

Example: We've seen an enormous _____ (*n*) in the number of businesses using the Web.

a) E-commerce is a _____ (__) recent phenomenon.

b) The virus could destroy the _____ (__) database.

c) Online _____ (__) is becoming an increasing problem in e-commerce.

d) Researchers have _____ (__) that some computer users are spending up to 15 hours a day at their machines.

e) The installation of anti-spam software can _____ (__) unwanted e-mails reaching your computer.

f) This network system is _____ (__) sound.

g) There are simple measures you can take to _____ (__) becoming a victim of computer fraud.

h) The _____ (__) of organised criminal gangs targeting the Internet is not in doubt.

i) Criminals have developed _____ (__) sophisticated techniques to bypass computer security systems.

j) Most experts recommend _____ (__) security checks.

k) The university should _____ (__) more computer facilities for students.

Study tip: It can be useful to link new words with any related synonyms and antonyms that you know.

2.3 Now complete the sentences above with words from the table in Exercise 2.1. In the case of verbs, pay attention to the ending required, e.g., ~s, ~ed,~ing, etc.

Example: We've seen an enormous _growth_ (n) in the number of businesses using the Web.

Task 3: Words belonging to two or more classes

We noted in Task 1 that some words can belong to more than one word class. You may only know them as belonging to one class.

Example: *average* can be a noun, a verb or an adjective

● *In the years between 1982 and 1988, the economy grew at an **average** of nearly three percent per year. (n)*

● *Inflation **averaged** just under 2.8 percent per year. (v)*

● *The **average** cost of making a movie has risen by 15 percent. (adj)*

3.1 Use a monolingual dictionary to check the different word classes these words belong to.

Word	Word class
excess	noun, adjective
stem	
match	
influence	
lack	

Word	Word class
rank	
spare	
joint	
risk	
sample	

Study tip: Experiment with words by saying them silently to yourself or out loud and by linking them with real or mental images.

3.2 The words from the table above appear in the following sentences. Which word class do they belong to in these sentences?

Example: A decline in soft drinks sales has left the industry with **spare** capacity. (adj)

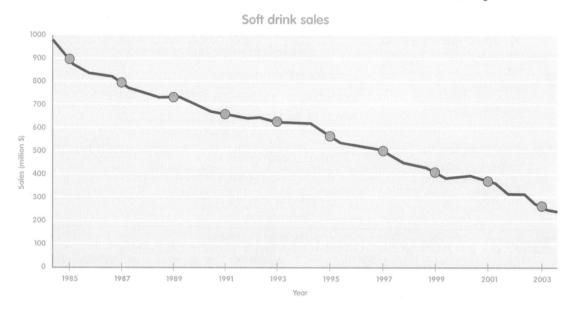

Soft drink sales

a) Many factories saw **excess** production during the first six months of the year. (——)

b) However, **lack** of investment has been the major problem for many companies in the drinks sector. (——)

c) This company's performance has not **matched** that of its competitors. (——)

d) Pepsi-Cola **ranks** as one of the world's biggest manufacturers. (——)

e) Many companies have entered into **joint** venture agreements with Eastern European companies. (——)

f) The drink is regularly **sampled** to check its quality. (——)

g) Many of the drinks industry's current problems **stem** from the bad weather in the peak sales season. (——)

h) External factors have a strong **influence** on sales in the drinks industry. (——)

i) The company took a calculated **risk** to appoint a man without management experience to such a senior post. (——)

3.3 If you feel you need more practice, continue the exercise you did in Exercise 3.1. Use a monolingual dictionary to check the different word classes these words belong to.

Word	Word class	Word	Word class
net	noun, verb, adjective, adverb	support	
experience		ideal	
rates		border	
double		prompt	
essential		blame	

3.4 Which word class do the words belong to in these sentences?

Example: The hotel group's chief executive told bankers that the March 31 accounts would show **net** assets had risen to £635 million compared with £385 million previously. (adj)

a) In the past five years the company has **experienced** a sharp upturn in sales. (___)

b) The group **rates** very highly in all surveys of luxury hotels worldwide. (___)

c) The number of business clients has nearly **doubled** over the past five years. (___)

d) Easy access to the airport is regarded as **essential** by most business clients. (___)

e) We **support** the idea of building hotels in downtown business centres. (___)

f) The hotel is situated in an **ideal** location, which is convenient both for the airport and the nearby business centre. (___)

g) Furthermore, it is only a few miles from the **border**, making it a suitable venue for clients intending to travel by car to other countries in the region. (___)

h) Staff will always deal **promptly** with any complaints. (___)

i) The fall in business last year was **blamed** on the strike by air traffic controllers. (___)

Study tip: Allocate time during your week to review new words from these activities.

Task 4: Review time

4.1 Complete these exercises about word class.

1 Which word classes do these words belong to?

a) advanced, elementary, entire, normal, academic: _____

b) develop, prevent, avoid, provide, spend: _____

c) size, performance, explanation, security, existence: _____

d) frequently, particularly, basically, highly: _____

2 Which two word classes can these words belong to?

a) influence: (___) and (___)

b) match: (___) and (___)

c) joint: (___) and (___)

d) lack: (___) and (___)

Study tip: When you find a word you have recently learnt in an academic text, use the context to ensure you are clear about its meaning.

4.2 Complete the gaps to write a summary of what you have learnt.

Knowledge of word class helps understanding of how to use _____ effectively. The best way to understand what word class a word _____ to is to read it in the context of a _____ or a paragraph. It is helpful to know that some words can belong to two or _____ word classes. For example, *prompt* can be a noun, a _____ or an adjective and *spare* can be a _____, a verb or an adjective.

4.3 Look again at the tasks in this unit and write down any new words (or phrases) you have learnt. Make sure you record which word class or word classes the words belong to. You may find it useful to record sentences in which the words occur.

Example:

New word	**Example sentence**
experience (noun and verb)	The company **experienced** a downturn in sales.

Make your own notes here.

_____
_____
_____
_____
_____
_____
_____
_____
_____
_____
_____
_____
_____
_____
_____
_____
_____
_____
_____
_____
_____
_____
_____

Study tip: It is always useful to find someone to study new words with.

3 Word families & word parts

This unit will help you:
- build your vocabulary by learning different members of word families;
- look at common prefixes and suffixes which are used to form different words, e.g., ~al as a suffix to form adjectives like *parental*, *economical* or ~ion as a suffix to form nouns like *restriction*;
- look at some common word parts which will help you identify the meanings of unknown words, e.g., ~port~ as in *export*, *portable*, etc.

Introduction

> **Study tip:** Learning vocabulary linked to one topic helps memorisation.

Look at the sentences below.

Of all the ideas for improving education, few are as simple or attractive as **reducing** the number of pupils per teacher.

Class-size **reduction** has lately developed from a subject of primarily academic interest to a key political issue.

The most obvious drawback to class-size **reduction** is the huge cost.

The state of California, for example, has been spending more than $1.5 billion annually over the past several years **to reduce** class size to 20 or fewer for children in the four- to seven-year-old bracket.

Source: Slaght, J., Harben, P., and Pallant, A. (2006). *English for Academic Study: Reading and Writing Source Book*. Reading: Garnet Education.

As you can see, different forms of the word *reduce* are used here; the noun *reduction* and the verb *to reduce*. The words are part of the same word family. In these sentences, the different members of the family are used to connect ideas within the text. Knowing different members of word families will give you another way of connecting ideas in your own written texts.

Look at another example of how different members of the same word family can be used to link together ideas and information in a text.

As we showed earlier, attitudes towards **children** were changing, in the upper levels of society at least, by the seventeenth century, but **childhood**, as people think of it today, did not become clearly established for most of the population until the nineteenth century. Two key changes during this century were the restriction of **child** labour by the Factory Acts and the development of compulsory education, which was gradually lengthened until the school-leaving age reached 16 in 1972. These changes created a space for **childhood** between infancy and adulthood and kept **children** in the parental home for a longer period.

Source: Fulcher, J., & Scott, J. (1999). *Sociology*. Oxford: Oxford University Press.

In this text, different members of the word family *child* are used; *child*, *childhood* and *children*.

Look at some of the other words from this text and at their family members.

Word in text	Other family members
parental (adj.)	parent (noun)
restriction (noun)	restrict (verb), restrictive (adj.)
lengthen (verb)	long (adj.), length (noun)
development (noun)	developmental (adj.), developmentally (adverb), develop (verb)
changes (noun)	change (verb)

Notice that some of the family members look very different from each other, for example, *long* and *lengthen*.

In other word families, the form of the words is the same but the word class is different, for example, *change* is both a noun and a verb. The form is the same.

> **Study tip:** There are many ways to link ideas and information – See *English for Academic Study: Writing*.

Task 1: Words that do not change

1.1 Look at the verbs below and tick (✓) which of them have the same form as the noun. If the noun has a different form, write it in the table. If you are not sure, check in a good monolingual dictionary.

Verb	Same form or different?
change	✓
restrict	restriction
employ	
cause	
offer	
depend	
claim	
decrease	

Verb	Same form or different?
respond	
influence	
suggest	
aim	
argue	
risk	
waste	

Task 2: Suffixes

In Unit 2 you looked at word classes. It is sometimes possible to recognise what class a word belongs to by looking at its ending, e.g., ~ion, ~ate, ~al, ~our, ~ive, ~ise, ~ly, ~ence, ~ity, ~ness.

Examples:

- restrict**ion**, develop**ment** = nouns
- development**al**, parent**al** = adjectives
- developmental**ly** = adverb

> **Language note:** Some suffixes provide meaning in addition to indicating word class. *Painful* and *painless* are both adjectives of the noun *pain*, but have different meanings.

2.1 Put the words in the box into the table below according to their word class.

activate	appropriate	~~behaviour~~	calculate	development	difference
economical	equality	formation	gradually	~~realise~~	social

Nouns	Verbs	Adjectives	Adverbs
behaviour	realise		

2.2 Which suffixes suggest which word classes? Refer back to the previous exercise and to the Introduction to this unit and complete this table with suffixes which suggest word classes.

Nouns	Verbs	Adjectives	Adverbs
~ion ~ment			

> **Study tip:** The suffixes above *can* indicate that words belong to a particular word class, but are *not* a guarantee of this. For example, the words *ritual* and *potential* end in ~al, but are both nouns and adjectives.

Task 3: Meaningful prefixes

In addition to suffixes at the end of words, which can indicate word class, we can look at word prefixes at the beginning of words. These prefixes do not tell us about the class of words but they can help us understand the meaning of words.

Example: prerequisite, preconceive, prefix

The words above all have the same prefix, *pre~*, which means 'before'.

> **Language note:** A prefix can be removed from a word and what remains is still a word, for example, the prefix *ir~* can be removed from these words: *irrelevant* (relevant), *irrational* (rational).

3.1 Complete the table with words beginning with the prefixes given.

Prefixes	Example words
mono~	monotone, monorail
bi~	bipolar, biannual
re~	
inter~	
anti~	
geo~	
post~	
micro~	
semi~	
sub~	
thermo~	

3.2 Match the meanings below to the prefixes from the table above.

Example:

    again, back   *re*

a) after, later   _____

b) exactly half, not complete   _____

c) connected with heat   _____

d) extremely small   _____

e) between   _____

f) under, a less important person or thing   _____

g) connected with (the) earth   _____

h) against, opposed to   _____

i) two, twice   _____

j) one, singular   _____

Task 4: Negative prefixes

Many words can be given a negative meaning by adding a prefix, for example,
*convenient – **in**convenient; agree – **dis**agree.*

4.1 Check the words in the list below in your dictionary and see which of these negative prefixes
are used with them: *dis~, in~, un~, ir~, ab~, il~, im~.*

Example:

    certainty   *uncertainty*

a) satisfactory   _____   **f)** normal   _____

b) efficient   _____   **g)** relevant   _____

c) likely   _____   **h)** legal   _____

d) appearance   _____   **i)** moral   _____

e) principled   _____   **j)** published   _____

> **Language note:** Not all words beginning with one of these prefixes has a negative meaning.
> For example: An *inbound* flight. To *implant* an artificial heart.

> **Language note:** The prefix *in~* is not normally used with words beginning with *b, l, m, p, r.*

Task 5: Family members that look different from each other

5.1 Match words from the left column with family members from the right column.

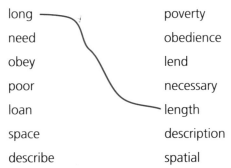

long   poverty

need   obedience

obey   lend

poor   necessary

loan   length

space   description

describe   spatial

Note: The words in Exercise 5.1 look very different from each other, but sometimes even when
the difference is not as great it can be difficult to find word family members in your dictionary.

Example: You will find the verb *vary* on one page of a monolingual dictionary but in many dictionaries you would have to look on a completely different page to find the family members *variable*, *variation* and *variant*.

If you want to find word family members, you may have to look at the stem of the word, e.g., *var~*, when you look for other related words.

Language note: Remember that for words ending in ~*y* this letter often changes to an ~*i* when a suffix is added, e.g., *easy – easier*.

Task 6: Complete word families

6.1 Complete the word family table below with the words in the box.

competition   decide   permit   economy   complicated   absence
competitive   complication   certainty   originate   decisive
economically   decisively   economise   origin   certainly

Nouns	Verbs	Adjectives	Adverbs
	compete		
decision			
permission, permit			
		economic, economical	
			originally
	complicate		
		absent	
		certain	

6.2 Complete the following sentences using a member of the word family given in brackets.

Example: Economists often argue that ____competition____ is good for the consumer. (compete)

a) It is an absolute _____ that the ruling party will win the forthcoming election. (certain)

b) In the manager's _____ the assistant manager will be in charge of the company. (absent)

c) Most people believe that high fuel prices are _____ damaging. (economy)

d) A photocopy of this certificate is not sufficient. You will have to bring the _____ document. (origin)

e) The _____ to make 20 percent of the workforce redundant was not taken lightly. (decide)

f) Photocopies may not be made without the _____ of the author. (permit)

g) The construction of the new road has been delayed as a result of legal _____. (complicate)

Task 7: Cohesion: Using nouns and verbs to connect ideas and information

7.1 In the following pairs of sentences you will need two forms of the same headword. Use different forms of the headwords in this box to complete the sentences below.

different   explain   difficult   argue   ~~believe~~   develop

Example: Supporters of Darwin's theories ____believe____ that human life evolved gradually over millions of years. This ____belief____ is strongly opposed by creationists.

a) They _____ the registration process in some detail. However, the _____ was rather complicated and several people failed to understand.

b) People react in _____ ways to dangerous situations. These _____ cannot simply be attributed to psychological factors.

c) There is a strong _____ that there is a link between violent computer games and violent behaviour. The manufacturers of such games _____ that their products do not influence people's behaviour, however.

d) Some elderly people find prepackaged foods _____ to open. The main _____ is that some of the materials used in packaging are quite tough.

e) Many studies have recorded how young children's language skills _____. The _____ of second-language skills in children is also of great interest to researchers.

Task 8: Word parts

In earlier tasks in this unit, we have seen that suffixes can give us information about word classes and that prefixes can give us some information about the meaning of words.

We can also find some non-detachable word parts which occur in a number of different words and which have related meanings. For example, the word part (or root) *phon(e)*, which means 'sound', is found in a number of different words whose meaning is connected to *sound*.

Examples: tele**phon**e, **phon**etics, micro**phone**, etc.

> **Study tip:** Non-detachable means it cannot be separated from the word and still leave a complete word. For example, if you separate *mem~* from *memory* what is left, *~ory*, is not a word. Contrast this with a prefix.

8.1 Look at the groups of words below and <u>underline</u> any common word parts.

Example: <u>mem</u>ory, <u>mem</u>orial, re<u>mem</u>ber, com<u>mem</u>orate

a) centenary, percentage, century

b) transport, portable, import, export

c) biology, psychology, geology

d) television, telephone, telescope

e) visual, vision, visible

f) prospect, respect, perspective, spectator

g) photograph, telephoto, photosynthesis

Study tip: You will often find word parts in words which do not have a meaning connection. For example, in *member*, *mem~* is not connected with 'keeping something in mind'.

8.2 Now match the word parts to their meanings.

Example:

keep in mind _____mem_____

a) light _____

b) far away _____

c) carry, move _____

d) watch, look at _____

e) one hundred _____

f) see _____

g) study of _____

Task 9: Review time

Study tip: Develop learning strategies that you use on a regular basis. The more you use them the more automatic they will become.

Look again at the tasks in this unit and write down any new words or phrases you have learnt. You may find it useful to write down phrases or sentences in which the words occur. You may also find it useful to write down the different members of the word family.

Example:

Word	Other members of word family
employ	employment, employer, employee, unemployed

Example sentences

The factory **employs** over 2,000 people.

Mexican law prohibits the **employment** of children under 14.

9.1 Now do the same for these words.

a) compete

b) compare

c) direct

d) prepare

e) depend

9.2 Now add further examples of your own from words in this unit.

4 Collocations

This unit will help you:
- see how different classes of words combine in English;
- learn some useful collocations.

Introduction

Collocations are the way that words combine in a language to produce natural-sounding speech and writing. For example, in English you say *tall person* but *high mountain*. It would not be normal to say *high person* or *tall mountain*.

Tall person is an example of an "adjective + noun" combination, but there are many other possible word combinations which we call collocations.

- verb + noun: *gain experience*
- noun + verb: *unemployment goes up*
- noun + noun: *interest rate*
- verb + adverb: *rise sharply*
- verb + preposition: *choose between two things*
- adjective + preposition: *safe from danger*
- preposition + noun: *in advance*

Here are some examples in a text.

> Today most psychologists agree not only that both nature and nurture **play important roles** but that they interact continuously to **guide development**. For example, we shall see in Chapter 12 that the development of many **personality traits**, such as sociability and emotional stability, appear to be influenced about equally by heredity and environment; similarly, we shall see in Chapter 15 that **psychiatric illnesses** can have both genetic and environmental determinants.

Source: Atkinson, R.L. et al. Interaction between nature and nurture. *Hildegard's Introduction to Psychology*, 13th edition, quoted in Slaght, J., Harben, P., Pallant, A. (2006). *English for Academic Study: Reading and Writing Source Book*. Reading: Garnet Education.

In this text you can see that the word *role* is used with the verb *play* and the adjective *important*. Knowing the words that collocate with *role* allows you to produce phrases like *play an important role*.

The other examples of collocations highlighted in the text above are:

- *guide development*   verb + noun
- *personality traits*   noun + noun
- *psychiatric illnesses*   adjective + noun

Study tip: For more on "noun + noun" combinations see Unit 5 – Word grammar

Language note: Another type of collocation which is present in the above text is *nature and nurture*: "noun + *and* + noun". These often have a fixed order and therefore you cannot write *nurture and nature*. Another example is *facts and figures* (not *figures and facts*)

How do I learn collocations?

You already know many collocations without realising it. For example, you will have learnt some of the following phrases in your earliest English lessons:

- *Turn on the light*   verb + noun
- *Have breakfast*   verb + noun
- *A beautiful day*   adjective + noun
- *Ask a question*   verb + noun
- *Happy Birthday*   adjective + noun

In other words, you will learn many collocations without consciously studying them. However, you can consciously learn more collocations by looking carefully at texts or by using a dictionary.

Study tip: Part of using a word properly is knowing what other words you can use it with.

Task 1: Learning from texts

1.1   Look at the following text and answer the questions that follow.

Because babies cannot explain what they are doing or tell us what they are thinking, developmental psychologists have had to design some very ingenious procedures to study the capacities of young infants. The basic method is to introduce some change in the baby's environment and observe his or her responses. For example, an investigator might present a tone or a flashing light and then see if there is a change in heart rate or if the baby turns its head or sucks more vigorously on a nipple. In some instances, the researcher will present two stimuli at the same time to determine if infants look longer at one than the other. If they do, it indicates that they can tell the stimuli apart and may indicate that they prefer one to the other.

Source: Atkinson, R.L. *et al.* Interaction between nature and nurture. *Hildegard's Introduction to Psychology*, 13th edition, quoted in Slaght, J., Harben, P., Pallant, A. (2006). *English for Academic Study: Reading and Writing Source Book.* Reading: Garnet Education.

1   What verbs are used before the following nouns?

Example:

| <u>design</u> | procedures |

a) _____   change

b) _____   responses

c) _____   stimuli

2 What adjectives are used with these nouns?

a) _____ psychologists

b) _____ procedures

c) _____ infants

d) _____ method

Language note: Note the stress on the verb *present* used in the above text falls on the second syllable, unlike the noun *present*, where the stress is on the first syllable.

Task 2: Using a dictionary to learn collocations

By studying the text in Exercise 1.1 you can be fairly confident that the following phrases are good collocations.

- *design ingenious procedures*
- *observe someone's responses*
- *introduce a change*
- *young infants*

However, you may not know what other words you could use with the nouns above. For example, what other verbs could you use with *procedures*? One way of finding out is by using your monolingual dictionary. Some dictionaries give you specific information about collocations.

Example:

Word	Adjectives used with the word	Verbs used with the word
problem (noun)	fundamental, major, real, serious, etc.	face, solve, create, pose, etc.

With this information you can be fairly confident that the following phrases would be correct.

- *pose a serious problem*
- *face a major problem*

In other cases the information may not be given explicitly in your dictionary, but by looking at the example sentences in the dictionary you can identify collocations.

Study tip: A headword in a dictionary may have more than one definition, but only one entry. These words are polysemes, i.e., the definitions are related rather than completely different.

Study tip: Use a comprehensive dictionary whenever possible, as some smaller dictionaries do not provide example sentences.

2.1 Look at the following example sentences and answer the questions that follow.

a) They are putting **pressure** on him to accept the job.

b) There is great **pressure** on the UN to take action.

c) The government is coming under **pressure** to hold a public enquiry into the matter.

d) I have no **doubts** at all about her ability to do the job.

e) Some people have expressed serious **doubts** over the government's economic policy.

f) There are still some **doubts** about his suitability for a senior position.

g) I am delighted to have the **opportunity** to present my ideas to such a distinguished audience.

h) There are now more **opportunities** for Eastern Europeans to find work in Western Europe.

i) I'd like to take this **opportunity** to thank you for your help in this matter.

Questions:

a) What verbs are used with the nouns *pressure, doubts, opportunities*?

b) When *pressure, doubts, opportunities* are followed by a preposition and noun, what are the prepositions?

c) When *pressure* and *opportunities* are followed by a verb phrase, what form does the verb take – "*to* + infinitive" or "verb + ~*ing*"?

You can use your answers to the different questions in Exercise 2.1 to build phrases.

Example:

put pressure on (someone to do something)

There is an opportunity (for someone to do something)

2.2 Write out the other phrases you can make by combining your answers to the questions in Exercise 2.1.

a) doubt

have no doubts about

b) pressure

c) opportunity

Study tip: The more you use a word the easier it will be to recall it when you need it.

2.3 Complete these sentences with a word in each gap. All the words you need are in your answers to Exercise 2.1.

Example: All he needs is an **opportunity** _to_ show his ability.

a) Career **opportunities** _____ young people have improved in the last 20 years.

b) There _____ several **opportunities** for experienced programmers and software designers.

c) He always _____ **pressure** on the sales team to achieve their targets.

d) The **pressure** _____ professionals in many walks of life is increasing day by day.

e) But there _____ no **doubt** that sensible investment will produce a good return.

f) My financial advisor is sure this is the best possible investment but I _____ my **doubts**.

Task 3: Verb + noun combinations

3.1 Look in a good monolingual dictionary and check which verbs are often used before these nouns.

Example: _make, have, cause_ _____ trouble

a) _____ (a) business

b) _____ an effort

c) _____ an impact

d) _____ a connection

e) _____ an effect

f) _require, have, provide_ _____ proof

g) _____ a gap

h) _improve, raise, meet, comply with_ _____ standards

i) _____ concern

Task 4: Verb + noun + preposition

4.1 Look again at the "verb + noun" combinations from Exercise 3.1. If they were followed by a noun phrase they would need a preposition as well. What prepositions would you need after the nouns in these sentences?

Example: We're having a lot of trouble _with_ the new software.

a) There is a widening gap _____ rich and poor countries.

b) Tariffs on agricultural products have a major impact _____ farmers in the developing world.

c) There is a great deal of concern _____ the continuing drought in parts of Africa.

d) Another dry winter could have a serious effect _____ this year's harvest.

e) Some people fail to see a connection _____ subsidies to farmers in the West and poverty in the developing world.

f) We need to do business _____ the people directly producing the goods.

Study tip: When you see a word you have been studying in an academic text or newspaper, look at the words it is used with.

Task 5: Adjective + noun

5.1 Look in your dictionary and check which adjectives are often used before these nouns.

Example: _slight, dramatic, significant_   increase

a) _____   problem

b) _____   supply

c) _____   standards

5.2 Look at these example sentences and underline the adjectives that are used with the highlighted nouns.

a) The main **purpose** of this meeting is to set sales targets for next year.

b) His sole **purpose** in attending the meeting was to gather information.

c) Everyone was there for a particular **purpose**.

d) There is a growing **demand** for organic food.

e) In the past five years there has been a huge **demand** for exotic fruit in the UK.

f) Recent **studies** show that the costs of importing food over long distances far outweigh the benefits.

g) The advice she gave was entirely of a practical **nature**.

h) It is human **nature** to want to be successful.

i) There is growing public **concern** about the high cost of public transport.

j) This issue will be discussed in greater **detail** in the next section.

Task 6: Adverb + verb, adverb + adjective

6.1 Underline the adverbs in these sentences and then answer the questions that follow.

a) If we manage natural resources more effectively, the quality of human life could be greatly improved.

b) Regular exercise can significantly reduce your risk of suffering a heart attack.

c) A balanced diet is especially important.

d) The maximum permitted daily dose is clearly stated on the label.

e) Some patients experience a recurrence of the symptoms as the effectiveness of the drug gradually decreases.

f) A knowledge of one or more foreign languages would be particularly useful for this position.

g) It is becoming increasingly difficult to find people with adequate linguistic skills.

h) Online shopping is a relatively recent phenomenon.

i) The problem was probably caused by a computer virus.

j) Such viruses can spread rapidly and affect millions of computers in minutes.

k) She strongly disagreed with the decision to replace all the hardware.

l) Using this system is comparatively easy and the basics can be learned in just a few hours.

Questions:

a) Which adverbs are used with verbs and what verbs are they used with?

Example: effectively: manage effectively

b) Which adverbs are used with adjectives and which adjectives are they used with?

Example: especially: especially important

Task 7: Review time

7.1 Complete these exercises using collocations from this unit.

a)

Verb	+	Noun
have		trouble
_____		an effect
_____		resources
_____		a connection

b)

Verb	+	Noun	+	Preposition
have		trouble		_____
have		an impact		_____
do		business		_____

c) Adjective   +   Noun

widening   _____

sole   _____

growing   _____

d) Verb   +   Adverb

_____   significantly

_____   rapidly

_____   clearly

e) Adverb   +   Adjective

_____   difficult

_____   important

_____   useful

7.2 Look again at the tasks in this unit and write down any new words (or phrases) you have learnt. Make sure you record which word class or word classes the words belong to. You may find it useful to write down phrases or sentences in which the words occur.

Example

Word	Example sentence
gap	There is a widening **gap** between the rich and the poor.

Make your own notes here.

_____

_____

_____

_____

_____

_____

_____

_____

_____

_____

_____

_____

_____

_____

_____

_____

_____

_____

Word grammar

This unit will help you:
- see how certain key words connect to each other;
- see how these key words connect to the rest of the sentence.

Introduction

When you study grammar you learn about how different word classes behave in general. When you use individual words, however, you realise that not all words in the same word class behave in the same way. The way that words connect to each other and to the rest of the sentence varies from one word to another.

For example, there is one set of verbs that commonly occurs with "*that* + clause", such as *think, say, know*, as in the sentence *Most people* think that *small classes help students learn more effectively.*

There is another set of verbs that commonly occurs with "*to* + clause", such as, *want, seem, like*. For example, *Although the government* wants to *decrease class sizes, they are unable to find enough money to implement such policies.*

Task 1: Combining nouns

Academic texts are very rich in noun combinations, so it is important to understand the different ways that nouns combine.

1.1   Look at the following text and answer the questions.

> For many years after the discovery of America, the movement of free migrants from Europe was steady but quite small: transport costs were high, conditions harsh and the dangers of migration great. In 1650, a free migrant's passage to North America cost nearly half a year's wages for a farm labourer in southern England.

Source: Slaght, J., Harben, P., Pallant, A. (2006). Economics Focus: On the Move. In *English for Academic Study: Reading and Writing Source Book*. Reading: Garnet Education.

a)   What examples are there of two nouns (or noun phrases) connected by a preposition?

Example: *the discovery of America*

b)   What examples are there of two nouns connected using apostrophe (') + *s*?

Example: *a free migrant's passage*

c)   What examples are there of "noun + noun" combination without a preposition?

Example: *transport costs*

Task 2: Noun followed by noun complement clause

There are a number of nouns that are followed by "*that* + clause". For example:

- *It is my **belief (that)** we will find a solution to this problem.*
- *He had a **theory that** many medical conditions were caused by viruses.*

Note: In the first example, *that* is optional and is therefore shown in brackets.

The function of the noun clause is to give meaning to the noun. As you can see in the two examples above, the clauses following the words *belief* and *theory* provide the content, or meaning. This is why they are called "noun complement clauses".

Look at the following extract. Note that there can be other words between the noun and the noun complement clause.

> the seventeenth-century British philosopher John Locke rejected the prevailing **notion** of his day **that babies were miniature adults**

Source: Atkinson, R.L. *et al*. Interaction between nature and nurture. *Hildegard's Introduction to Psychology*, 13th edition, quoted in Slaght, J., Harben, P., Pallant, A. (2006). *English for Academic Study: Reading and Writing Source Book*. Reading: Garnet Education.

2.1 In the table below there are seven nouns. Check them in your dictionary and tick (✓) which of them can be followed by "*that* + clause".

Word	*that* + clause	Not followed by *that* + clause
belief	✓	
notion		
theory		
view		
idea		
fact		
suggestion		

Task 3: Other noun patterns

3.1 Look at the highlighted nouns in the following sentences. Identify which of the four types each one is, depending on whether it is followed by:

1 prepositions (to connect the following nouns or gerunds);

2 *that* + clause;

3 *to* + infinitive;

4 "*wh~* word + clause" or "preposition + *wh~* word + clause".

Write the number in the box provided.

	1	The company is introducing a new **system** for dealing with telephone enquiries.
a)		The prime minister rejected **claims** that he had acted without authority.
b)		The **suggestion** that a new road should be built through the area did not go down well with environmental groups.
c)		Over the past 35 years, **hundreds** of studies and **analyses** of existing data have focused on class size.
d)		Many countries aspire to a more democratic **system** of government.
e)		The **reason** why these laws are needed is to protect the public from violent individuals.
f)		People give many different **reasons** for wanting to emigrate.
g)		This raises the whole **question** of the average wage and the standard of living in this country.
h)		The purpose of the survey is to find more effective **ways** of evaluating job satisfaction.
i)		Some companies set **limits** on the amount of money employees may claim for travel expenses.
j)		There's no **limit** on the **amount** of money that can be exported from the country.
k)		There was no **doubt** that this was one of the most important discoveries in the **history** of medical research.

E

> **Language note:** A gerund operates in the same way as a noun, e.g., it can be the subject or the object of a sentence. It has the same form as the present participle, e.g., *smoking*.

3.2 Look at the type 1 sentences in Exercise 3.1 above and circle the preposition used to connect the highlighted noun to the following noun or gerund.

3.3 If you feel you need further practice in identifying noun patterns, continue with the following sentences in the same way as in Exercise 3.1 above.

a) ☐ One **solution** to this problem is for animals to be vaccinated against the disease.

b) ☐ All **attempts** to control the spread of the disease have failed.

c) ☐ Many people have a **suspicion** that the government is attempting to cover up the truth about the extent of the problem.

d) ☐ There is a **risk** that the outbreak may spread further and affect other parts of the country.

e) ☐ Regular exercise can help reduce the **risk** of heart disease.

f) ☐ Poor diet combined with lack of exercise is the **root** of many people's health problems.

g) ☐ You need formal **permission** to take copies of certain books out of the library.

h) ☐ The government has announced its **intention** to introduce a new peace plan in an attempt to end more than 20 years of conflict in the region.

i) ☐ The proposed peace plan includes a **mechanism** to share power between the two main parties.

j) ☐ They have examined the **extent** to which the two communities have been able to coexist in the past.

k) ☐ The **way** that some people react to members of the other community varies greatly.

l) ☐ At the present time there seems to be no **way** to bring the two sides together.

3.4 Look at the type 1 sentences in Exercise 3.3 above and circle the preposition used to connect the highlighted noun to the following noun or gerund.

Task 4: Noun + noun

We have already seen three combinations of nouns without prepositions, in the Introduction and Exercise 1.1: *class size, transport costs, farm labourer.*

Here are three more examples:

- *school subjects*
- *achievement levels*
- *classroom equipment*

> **Language note:** It is not possible to combine all nouns in this direct way but "noun + noun" combinations are very common in academic texts.

4.1 Check in your dictionary and find more nouns that can be used in combination with the following nouns (either before or after).

Example: government _figures, employees, spokesman, policy_

a) market _____

b) computer _____

c) problem _traffic, drug, health, behaviour, alcohol_

d) company _____

e) figure/figures _____

f) rate _____

Task 5: Adjectives and what follows them

As we saw in Unit 4: Collocations, adjectives are used before nouns. However, they are also used in other positions and in other ways. Look at the way the adjective _important_ is used in the following sentences.

- The experience taught him an **important** lesson.

- Good health is more **important** than money.

- It is **important** to explain the risks of the operation to the patient.

- It is **important** that everyone understands the dangers involved.

In the first sentence, _important_ is used before the noun. In the second sentence, it is used after the verb, but it is talking about the noun _health_, the subject of the sentence. In the third and fourth sentences, _important_ is used to comment on what comes after it, e.g., _explain the risks to the patient._ Another way of saying this would be _Explaining risks to the patient is important._

Notice that in the third sentence _important_ is followed by "_to_ + infinitive", whereas in the fourth sentence it is followed by "_that_ + clause".

> **Study tip:** Not all adjectives can be used in the four ways that the adjective _important_ can. As with nouns, you have to learn which adjectives can be used in particular ways.

5.1 Look at the highlighted adjectives in the following sentences. Identify which of the three types they are, depending on whether they are followed by:

1 _that_ + clause

2 _to_ + infinitive

3 preposition + noun phrase

a) ☐ Different vitamins are **necessary** for a healthy diet.

b) ☐ The new situation made it **necessary** to rethink the whole plan.

c) ☐ It's **difficult** to see how we can save more money without cutting jobs.

d) ☐ That's rather **difficult** for me to explain.

e) ☐ The Internet makes it **possible** for many people to work from home.

f) ☐ It is **possible** that one day humans might live on other planets.

g) ☐ It soon became **clear** that the situation was out of control.

h) ☐ It was **clear** to all of us that it was becoming dangerous.

i) ☐ The building of wind farms is **likely** to be unpopular with local residents.

j) ☐ It seems **likely** that supplies of natural gas will run out in the near future.

> **Study tip:** Some monolingual dictionaries will give explicit information on how to use adjectives, e.g., with the adjective *familiar* you will probably find *familiar (+ to)*. This means *familiar* can be followed by the preposition *to* and a noun (e.g., *This place seems very familiar to me.*). In other cases you can get information by looking closely at the example sentences.

5.2 Look at the type 3 sentences in Exercise 5.1 above and identify the preposition used to connect the highlighted adjective to the following noun phrase.

5.3 Look at the sentences in Exercise 5.1 again. Which highlighted adjectives can be used immediately before nouns?

5.4 Check these adjectives in your dictionary and answer the questions that follow.

common certain customary bound useful

a) Which of the above adjectives can be used in this pattern?

 It is _____ for someone to do something.

b) Which of the above adjectives can be used immediately before a noun?

 _____

 _____

c) Which of the above adjectives can be used with "*that* + clause"?

 _____

 _____

d) Which of the above adjectives can be immediately followed by "*to* + infinitive"?

 _____

 _____

Task 6: Verbs and verb patterns

Verbs can also be followed by different patterns. Look at these two examples:

In general, the ability to **distinguish** among smells has a clear adaptive value: it helps infants **avoid** noxious substances, thereby **increasing** their likelihood of survival.

It is hard to **know** how much of the performance **stems** from other factors, such as a supportive home.

Source: Atkinson R.L. *et al.* Interaction between nature and nurture. *Hildegard's Introduction to Psychology*, 13th edition, quoted in Slaght, J., Harben, P., Pallant, A. (2006). *English for Academic Study: Reading and Writing Source Book*. Reading: Garnet Education.

The highlighted verbs in the texts above are followed by different patterns.

- *Avoid* and *increasing* are both followed by noun phrases – *noxious substances* and *their likelihood of survival.*

- *Stems* and *distinguish* are followed by prepositions + noun phrases – *from other factors* and *among smells.*

- *Know* is followed by a *wh~* word (*how much*) + clause – *how much of the performance stems from other factors.*

These are only some of the patterns that can be used with verbs. You will find other patterns as you study verbs in examples of text, or in a monolingual dictionary. For example, *know* can be followed by:

- noun phrase

- preposition + noun phrase

- (*that*) + clause

- *wh~* word + clause

For the verbs highlighted in the extracts above, only the verb *know* can be followed by all of these patterns.

> **Language note:** A noun phrase is a phrase with a noun (or pronoun) as head. Examples:
> - *a substance*
> - *this substance*
> - *a chemical substance*

> **Study tip:** Individual verbs can be followed by different patterns. You have to learn which patterns can be used with each verb.

Task 7: Transitive and intransitive verbs

Labelling verbs as transitive or intransitive is one of the most basic ways of categorising verbs.

Transitive verbs can be used in the following two ways:

- With a direct object: *Many British children spend hours **playing** computer games.*
- In the passive: *The rugby match **was watched** by over 60,000 people.*

Intransitive verbs <u>cannot</u> be used with a direct object and <u>cannot</u> be used in the passive. For example, you can say *It exists*, but you cannot say:

- *it exists something* or *something is existed.*

7.1 Look at the highlighted verbs in the following text and decide whether they are transitive or intransitive.

> The surge of interest in smaller classes has **spurred** fresh analyses of the largest, most conclusive study to date, which **took place** in Tennessee in the late 1980s. At the same time, new data **are flowing** from various initiatives, **including** the California programme and a smaller one in Wisconsin. These results and analyses are finally **offering** some tentative responses to the questions that researchers must **answer** before legislators can **come up with** policies that make educational and economic sense: Do small classes in fact **improve** school achievement? If they do, at what age-level do they **accomplish** the greatest good? What kind of students **gain** the greatest benefit, and most importantly, how great is the benefit?

Source: Atkinson, R.L. *et al.* Interaction between nature and nurture. *Hildegard's Introduction to Psychology,* **13th edition,** quoted in Slaght, J., Harben, P., Pallant, A. (2006). *English for Academic Study: Reading and Writing Source Book.* Reading: Garnet Education.

Example: spurred   *transitive*

a) took place   _____

b) are flowing   _____

c) including   _____

d) offering   _____

e) answer   _____

f) come up with   _____

g) improve   _____

h) accomplish   _____

i) gains   _____

7.2 You can use your dictionary to find out whether verbs are transitive or not. Different dictionaries use different symbols to indicate this. For example:

	Transitive	Intransitive
Oxford Advanced Learners' Dictionary:	[VN] i.e., verb + noun	[V] i.e., verb
Longman Dictionary of Contemporary English:	[T]	[I]
Macmillan English Dictionary for Advanced Learners:	[T]	[I]

7.3 Look at the list of verbs below. Some are always transitive and some are always intransitive. Complete the table with these verbs.

| belong | describe | exist | interfere | lack | mention |
| remain | result | rise | suggest |

Transitive	Intransitive
present include	appear

Language note: Some intransitive verbs can become transitive if a preposition is added, for example, *result: A sudden change in temperature will inevitably* result *in rain.* The verbs *belong* and *interfere* can both be followed by preposition and noun phrases.

7.4 Check the verbs *belong* and *interfere* in your dictionary and complete these sentences with the correct prepositions.

a) These cars look as if they belong _____ a different era.

b) Anxiety can interfere _____ children's performance at school.

7.5 The following verbs are sometimes transitive and sometimes intransitive. This may depend on the different meanings of the verbs.

| believe | govern | spread | succeed | tend |

Look at these example sentences from monolingual dictionaries and decide if the highlighted verbs are being used transitively (VT) or intransitively (VI).

Example: They questioned the prime minister's ability to **govern**.   _(VI)_

a) The disease quickly **spread** from animals to humans.   _____

b) Under the current economic conditions the reform programme simply cannot **succeed**.   _____

c) People **tend** to save more money as they get older.   _____

d) A team of paramedics **tended** the most seriously injured.   _____

e) I **believed** everything they told me.   _____

f) There are new laws which **govern** the import of animal products.   _____

g) They are hiring extra staff to **spread** the workload.   _____

Task 8: Verbs followed by "*that* + clause"

8.1 Study the following example sentences.

- *She **argued** that they needed more money to complete the project.*
- *Both sides firmly **believe** that an agreement is now possible.*
- *Police now **know** that the crime was committed by someone known to the victim.*

Check these verbs in your dictionary and indicate which of them can be followed by *that* or "*that* + clause". Good monolingual dictionaries normally give you the information explicitly like this:

believe *[V (that)]: People used to believe (that) the world was flat.*

Verb	*that* + clause	Not followed by *that* + clause
decrease		✓
behave		
state		
consider		
admit		
introduce		

8.2 Look through these example sentences and underline any verb that is followed by "*that* + clause".

a) Smoking is widely believed to cause a range of medical problems.

b) Ten years ago it was finally agreed that tobacco advertising would be banned.

c) All the evidence suggests that the number of people smoking is falling steadily.

d) It is worth mentioning that teenagers in particular need to be warned about the dangers of smoking.

e) Some companies claim that their products can help people to stop smoking.

f) But some researchers have discovered that the chemicals in certain products actually increase nicotine dependence rather than reducing it.

g) In the US, smokers have come to accept that they can no longer smoke in any public place or workplace.

h) Some people have expressed concern about the widespread availability of cheap cigarettes from abroad.

i) She admitted that she smoked even though the job description explicitly called for non-smokers.

j) Researchers claim to have discovered a harmless tobacco substitute.

Task 9: Verbs followed by *wh~* words

9.1 Study the following examples of sentences followed by "*wh~* word + clause" or "*wh~* word + infinitive".

- *We need to **discover what** our competitors are doing.*
- *The police asked him to **explain what** he was doing in the victim's apartment.*
- *Psychologists began to **ask whether** learning and experience play an important role in such differences.*
- *It is sometimes difficult to **decide whether** to invest money or save it.*

All the verbs in the table below can be followed by different "*wh~* words + clause". Check the verbs in your dictionary and complete the table by writing in the *wh~* words they are used with.

Verb	Wh~ word
doubt	*whether*
consider	
determine	
explain	
decide	
describe	
realise	
discuss	

Study tip: Some dictionaries will give examples of which *wh~* words to use with a verb, e.g., (verb + *whether/if* + clause), but at other times you may have to study the example sentences to identify the *wh~* word.

9.2 For the pattern used in Exercise 9.1, the word order is not the same as it would be for questions introduced by *wh~* words. Compare the following:

Question:
What are our competitors doing?

Verb followed by *wh~* word:
(We need to) discover what our competitors are doing.
(complement +) verb + *wh~* word + subject + verb)

9.3 Rearrange these sets of jumbled words to complete sentences with "verb + *wh~* words + clauses". The first word in each sentence is in bold to help you begin.

Example: will explain / **The** secretary / the forms / you have to / fill in / how

The secretary will explain how you have to fill in the forms.

a) **We** / for next year / we want / to discuss / what kind of strategy / need

b) existed / the document / doubted / **They** / whether / had ever

c) why / will also describe / difficult / I still find it / **I** / to accept his explanation

d) **We** / we should update / our advice to visitors / whether / are considering

e) **People** / have / what / with their own money / a right to decide / they should do

Task 10: Review time

10.1 Follow the instructions and write the words.

a) Write three verbs that can be followed by *that*.

b) Write three verbs that can be followed by *wh~* words.

c) Write three nouns that can be followed by *that*.

d) Write three adjectives that can be followed by *that*.

e) Write three adjectives that can be followed by "*to* + infinitive".

10.2 Look again at the tasks in this unit and write down any new words (or phrases) you have learnt. You may find it useful to write down phrases or sentences in which the words occur.

Example:

Word	Example phrase
dissatisfaction	express dissatisfaction with

Make your own notes here.

Part 2: Academic Word List

In these units we will be studying the frequent word families which are listed in the Academic Word List Sublists 1–5 (see Appendix for full version of all the sublists).

You will look at the following aspects:

- Meanings of words
- Multi-meaning words
- Word classes
- Word families
- Prefixes
- Collocations
- Word grammar
- Review time

The first two tasks will establish the meaning of the words, before looking at them in more detail in a similar way that you studied the General Service List words in Units 1 to 5 of the book.

Each unit ends with a word list containing words and phrases from the unit that occur frequently in academic English. These do not neccessarily correspond with the Academic Word List in the Appendix.

6 AWL – Sublist 1

This unit will help you:
- familiarise yourself with the word families in AWL Sublist 1;
- practise understanding and using these words in context.

Task 1: Meanings of words

1.1 Study the words in bold in the extracts below and then do the matching exercise that follows.

Education

a) The most obvious drawback to class-size reduction is the huge cost. It **requires** more teachers, more classrooms and more classroom equipment and resources.

b) Some studies have shown that the level of academic achievement amongst primary school children **varies** greatly depending on class size.

c) According to one source, the introduction of new secondary school examinations is **proceeding** smoothly.

d) Educationalists and school administrators are attempting to develop a common **approach** to controversial issues such as selection and streaming.

e) The growing popularity of the subject is **evident** in the numbers of students wanting to study it.

f) If a child is still doing well years later, it is hard to know how much of the performance stems from other **factors**, such as a supportive home.

Health

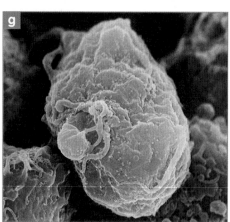

g) There is no reason to **assume** that a drug that can treat this particular virus will ever be found.

h) Minor changes in the patient's condition can **occur** without any obvious external signs.

i) The number of drugs currently **available** to treat this disease is strictly limited.

j) It is the medical researcher's job to **interpret** data gathered from thousands of hospital patients.

k) Most physicians believe we will **derive** great benefit from this new form of treatment.

l) He could see that the baby **responded** and was actively seeking his attention.

Match the words on the left with the definitions on the right. The first one has been done for you.

Example:

Word	Meaning
require	to need something or someone

Word	Meaning
require	to accept something as true, although you do not have proof
vary	easily seen or understood
proceed	to take actions or behaviours as having a particular meaning
approach	able to be found, bought or obtained
occur	one of the things that causes a situation or influences the way it happens
evident	to carry on doing something that has already started
assume	to need something or someone
respond	to happen
factor	a way of dealing with a situation or problem
available	to obtain or come from another source
interpret	to say or do something in reaction to something else
derive	to change or be different in different circumstances

Language note: If you use a dictionary to look up the word *approach* you will see that it is a polyseme, i.e., it has many related meanings.

Language note: The pronunciation of *proceeds* changes if you use the word as a verb or as a noun.

1.2 Complete the pairs of sentences below with the words from Exercise 1.1. In each pair you need the same word for both sentences. In the case of verbs, a different ending may be needed for the word, e.g., ~s, ~ed, ~ing. In the case of nouns you have to decide whether the singular or plural form is appropriate.

Example:

Information about this product is freely _____available_____ on the Internet.

Updates are _____available_____ from our website.

a) I think we can reasonably _____ that these coins date from the Roman period.

We can _____ that more artefacts will be found in this area but we cannot be certain.

b) Distances from the accommodations to the university _____ from two kilometres to six kilometres.

Journey times may _____ slightly, depending on the time of day.

c) It soon became _____ from her appearance that she was seriously ill.

It was _____ from the symptoms that she was suffering from an infection.

d) People often _____ his reserved manner as rudeness.

We will need someone to _____ for us on our trip to Russia as neither of us speaks a word of Russian.

e) It is clear that we need a completely different _____ to the problem of dealing with bad behaviour in schools.

The modern _____ to physical education in schools is very different to that of 20 or 30 years ago.

f) The recent increase in violent crime is mainly due to social and economic _____.

Finding a safe and relatively crime-free area is one of the key _____ for many people when buying a new home.

g) These symptoms _____ in a very small minority of patients.

Epidemics like this _____ very rarely.

h) This condition is very serious and _____ urgent treatment.

Any patient who _____ special diets should inform the hospital authorities.

i) The club is determined to _____ with its plans to build a new stadium despite the objections of local residents.

Before we _____ any further, we should define our terms.

Task 2: Multi-meaning words

> **Study tip:** Multi-meaning words were introduced in Unit 1 and are called "homonyms".

2.1 The words in the box below have at least two meanings. Look at how they are used in the sentences that follow and choose the correct meaning.

approach	area	authority	contract	establish	factor
	formula	interpret	issue	respond	source

Example:

Perhaps the most obvious sign of globalisation is in the economic **area**.

a) a particular part of a city, town, region or country

b) the amount of space covered by the surface of a place or shape

c) a particular subject or range of activities

Answer: c) a particular subject or range of activities

1 There have been many debates about the main influences on early human development throughout history, and even now many scientists are unable to agree about this **issue**.

    a) to officially give people something to buy or use, e.g., a passport

    b) a subject or problem people discuss or argue about

    c) a magazine or newspaper that is published at a particular time

2 He could see that the baby **responded** and was actively seeking his attention.

    a) to react well to a particular kind of treatment

    b) to reply to something either verbally or in writing

    c) to say or do something in reaction to something else

3 According to the latest figures, the economy **contracted** by 1.5 percent in the third quarter of last year.

    a) to become smaller

    b) to get an illness

    c) to formally agree to do something

4 The company's recent change of name has been the **source** of considerable confusion.

    a) someone or something that provides you with something you need

    b) the cause of a problem

    c) a document or person that you get information from

5 Both hereditary and environmental **factors** are important in human development.

    a) a particular level on a scale that measures how strong or large something is

    b) one of the things that causes a situation or influences the way it happens

    c) a number that can be divided evenly into another number

6 There is no magic **formula** that will solve this problem overnight.

    a) the symbols, numbers or letters used to represent a rule in mathematics or science

    b) the step-by-step procedure to use to solve a problem or achieve a result

    c) a list of the ingredients used to make things like medicines, drinks, etc.

7 The problem with trade and other aspects of globalisation is that there are no effective global **authorities** to control it.

   a) the power you have to make decisions or give other people instructions

   b) the police and other official organisations charged with enforcing laws or rules

   c) someone who is an expert in a particular subject

8 Different historians **interpret** the same historical events in different ways.

   a) to translate from one language into another

   b) to explain the meaning of something

   c) to take actions or behaviours as having a particular meaning

9 The government's **approach** to the question of illegal share-trading has been to ignore it.

   a) an offer or request to do something

   b) getting closer to a point in time or space

   c) a particular way of handling a situation or problem

10 They are carrying out research to **establish** exactly why changes in the hydrological cycle are taking place.

   a) to start a new company or organisation

   b) to secure a position by proving qualifications

   c) to find proof or facts that show that something is true

Task 3: Word classes

3.1 Check the following words in a dictionary. Then complete the table with the word class they belong to, i.e., noun, verb, adjective or adverb. Some words belong in more than one class.

Word	Word class	Word	Word class
focus	verb, noun	assess	
benefit		specific	
research		finance	
policy		consist of/in	
individual		identify	
function			

Study tip: For more information on word class, refer back to Unit 2: Word classes.

3.2 Decide what word class would fill each gap in the following sentences. Write *v* (verb), *n* (noun) or *adj* (adjective) in the brackets after each gap.

Example:

The _____ (_n_) of recent research has been on environmental issues.

Education

a) Most found evidence that smaller classes _____ (__) students, particularly at the youngest level.

b) Every baby has its own _____ (__) personality.

c) Much educational _____ (__) is carried out using secondary or library data.

d) A new government might adopt a _____ (__) of reducing spending on higher education.

e) The technique is being tried in classrooms to _____ (__) what effects it may have.

f) In some _____ (__) age and subject categories, such as 17-year-olds and science, performance actually decreased slightly.

Business and Finance

g) Police are trying to _____ (__) the person responsible for removing over $2 million from personal bank accounts.

h) The banking and _____ (__) sector is growing at an astonishing rate.

i) The government's policy is to allow banks to _____ (__) independently, free of external controls.

j) The alliance _____ (__) of a number of leading banks and financial institutions.

3.3 Now complete the sentences in Exercise 3.2 with words from the box in Exercise 3.1. In the case of verbs, a different ending may be needed for the word, e.g., ~s, ~ed, ~ing. In the case of nouns you may have to decide whether to use singular or plural forms.

If you change your mind about any word classes while doing this exercise, think about what led you to the original conclusion.

Example:

The ____focus____ (n) of recent research has been on environmental issues.

Task 4: Word families

Look at these two sentences.

> A 'world car' may have the same 'platform', but is sold with different shapes, colours and accessories to meet local **requirements**.

> Nevertheless, both regionalisation and globalisation **require** that more and more speakers and readers of local languages be multiliterate.

Source: Slaght, J., Harben, P., Pallant, A. (2006). *English for Academic Study: Reading and Writing Source Book*. Reading: Garnet Education.

The highlighted words, *require* and *requirement*, are both members of the same word family. Other words in the two sentences above also belong to word families.

Examples:

Word	Other members of the word family
different	difference (n), differ (v), differently (adv)
local	locality (n), localise (v), localisation (n)

4.1 Put the words in the box below into the table with other members of their families. Remember that you may not be able to complete every column for each word, but there may be some columns where there are two entries, e.g., *economic* and *economical* are both adjectives.

> ~~assessment~~   economy   vary   analysis   definition   significantly   responsive
> environmentally   indicate   creative   interpret   economically   response
> creation   variable   significant   indication

Nouns	Verbs	Adjectives	Adverbs
assessment	assess		
		economic economical	
variation			
	analyse		
significance			

Nouns	Verbs	Adjectives	Adverbs
		indicative	
	respond		
environment			
	create		
interpretation			
	define		

4.2 Choose the correct form of the word in brackets to complete the following sentences. In the case of verbs a different ending may be needed for the word, e.g., ~ed, ~ing, ~s. In the case of nouns you have to decide whether the singular or plural form is appropriate.

Example:

The average daily food ___requirement___ for an adult is between 2,000 and 3,000 calories. (require)

Health

a) Life expectancy in some areas of Scotland is up to ten years lower than in other parts of the UK – a _____ finding from a policy point of view. (significant)

b) There continue to be regional and social class _____ in diet and these can affect life expectancy significantly. (vary)

c) These food statistics can be _____ in a number of different ways. (interpret)

d) A poor diet in infancy can _____ numerous problems in later life. (create)

e) It is difficult to provide an accurate _____ of a healthy diet as this can vary from individual to individual. (define)

Environment

f) An _____ of data from Australia shows that the hole in the ozone layer over Antarctica is growing larger. (analyse)

September 24, 2001   September 24, 2002

g) The most recent _____ of the research suggests that human activities have had an influence on the global climate. (assess)

h) More recent studies _____ that ocean temperatures may rise by as much as 3°C over the next 50 years. (indicate)

i) Scientists have _____ by increasing the amount of research in this area. (respond)

j) The _____ effects of greenhouse gas emissions have been well-documented. (environment)

Task 5: Prefixes

The following prefixes are used with a number of the words from the AWL Sublist 1.

Prefix	Meaning
re~	again, e.g., *reheat = heat again*
in~	not, the opposite of, e.g., *incomparable = not comparable*
un~	not, the opposite of, e.g., *unhappy = not happy*
mis~	bad or badly, e.g., *mistreat = treat badly*
over~	too much, additional, e.g., *overheat = heat too much*
under~	not a sufficient amount, e.g., *underfed = not fed enough*

5.1 Which of the above prefixes can be used with the following words?

Example:

	variably	*invariably*
a)	significant	_____
b)	available	_____
c)	create	_____
d)	economical	_____
e)	interpret	_____
f)	responsive	_____
g)	assess	_____
h)	consistent	_____
i)	estimate	_____

5.2 Complete the following sentences using either:

- the word in brackets; or
- a prefix + the word in brackets.

In the case of verbs you should choose the correct ending, e.g., ~ed, ~ing, ~s. In the case of nouns you have to decide whether the singular or plural form is appropriate.

Example:

Old cars are very often _uneconomical_ . (economical)

Health

a) The disease mainly affects children, but can also _____ in adults. (occur)

b) Because of the high prices, many AIDS drugs are _____ in poor countries. (available)

c) Most doctors do not accept his interpretation because they say his results are _____ with the data produced. (consistent)

d) Compared with the problems people in the Third World have with diseases, our worries are _____ . (significant)

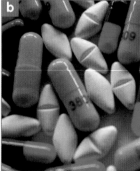

Business and Finance

e) The business community recognises that successful companies are those which are _____ to market changes. (responsive)

f) Some parts of the report could be _____ if people do not read it carefully. (interpret)

g) Numerous cases of online fraud have forced the major banks to _____ their security procedures. (assess)

h) We _____ how much the project would cost and ended up spending £10,000 more than we had planned. (estimate)

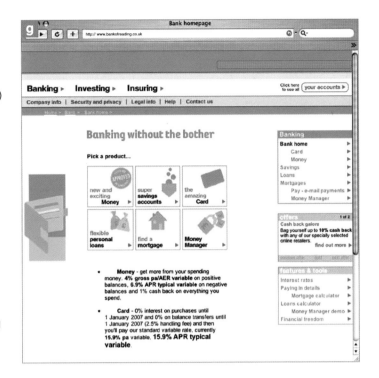

Task 6: Collocations

Verbs and nouns

Look at these "verb + noun" combinations that appear in this unit.

- *develop an approach*
- *derive benefit*

6.1 Match the verbs on the left with the nouns on the right to make combinations that can all be found in previous exercises in this unit.

Example:

require a special diet (Exercise 1.2, sentence h)

Verb	Noun
require	effects
interpret	research
meet	the person
carry out	requirements
adopt	data
identify	a special diet
assess	a policy

6.2 Choose one verb from the box that fits best with all the nouns in each group.

| adopt | ~~analyse~~ | assess | create | define | establish | estimate | play |

Example:

    analyse   data, results, problems, behaviour

a) _____ a role, a part

b) _____ a problem, a word, a term, a concept

c) _____ a plan, strategy, policy, an approach

d) _____ a company, cause, facts, a relationship

e) _____ cost, value, effects, the extent of something

f) _____ risk, performance, damage, effectiveness

g) _____ jobs, a system, a situation, wealth, products

6.3 Choose one noun from the box that fits best with all the verbs in each group.

| an analysis | benefit | ~~income~~ | issues | methods | theory |

Example:

    have, generate, supplement   _income_

a) discuss, address, raise _____

b) use, develop, adopt _____

c) support, test, develop _____

d) do, carry out, give _____

e) gain, bring, derive _____

Discovering collocations

You will learn a lot of collocations by paying attention to the way words are used in texts.

6.4 Look at the following sentences. Underline the verbs that combine with the nouns in bold to identify the different "verb + noun" and "noun + verb" combinations.

Example:

Many of the questions can be answered without <u>carrying out</u> any new **research**.

a) More **research** is needed into the ways in which infants acquire language.

b) Recent **research** has shown that human language is much older than we previously thought.

c) Our **analysis** shows that the proposed cost of the new building is unrealistic.

d) The report provides a detailed **analysis** of different designs for the building.

e) Scientists need to obtain more **data** before they can say for certain what the cause of the problem is.

f) All the **data** show that these diseases occur more frequently in industrialised societies.

g) The research involves collecting **data** from at least 20 random samples.

h) There is little or no scientific **evidence** to support this **theory**.

i) The prosecution failed to provide sufficient **evidence** to convict the accused.

j) After examining all the **evidence**, the judge agreed with the application.

k) Many studies of consumer behaviour have used the questionnaire **approach**.

l) If it wants to increase profits, the company needs to adopt a much more radical **approach**.

m) There are several **benefits** you can claim if you are disabled and unable to work.

n) Tourism has brought many **benefits** to people in this region.

Task 7: Word grammar

Discovering noun patterns

You have studied the following patterns in Unit 5: Word grammar. Exercise 7.1 will help you notice these patterns in the texts you read.

- noun + preposition, e.g., *function of*
- noun followed by *that*, e.g., *the theory that*
- noun + noun, e.g., *oil prices*

> **Study tip:** For more information about noun patterns, see Unit 4: Collocations.

7.1 Look at the nouns in bold in the sentences below and identify:

- what prepositions are used after the nouns;
- which nouns are followed by "*that* + clause";
- which "noun + noun" combinations are used.

Business and Finance

a) The data supports the **theory** that higher oil prices lead to higher inflation.

_____

_____

_____

b) Chapter 5 discusses the **theory** of marketing costs.

_____

_____

_____

c) The **assumption** that money invested in the stock market will always make a rapid profit is a long way from the truth.

_____

_____

_____

d) Companies will need to make **assumptions** about the knowledge of their customers.

_____

_____

_____

e) There is clear **evidence** of a link between price reductions and increased sales.

_____

_____

_____

f) There is much supporting **evidence** for this belief.

_____

_____

_____

g) The study found no **evidence** that consumers are willing to pay a price premium for high-quality products in this area.

_____

_____

_____

h) The **function** of the sales manager is to maintain regular contact with all the company's main customers and to identify new customers.

_____

_____

_____

i) Both sides regard regular communication as fundamental to the **process** of maintaining a good business relationship.

_____

_____

_____

j) The company is in the **process** of relocating to the north of England.

_____

_____

_____

k) Today's **approach** to sales and marketing is very different from 40 years ago.

_____

_____

_____

l) A systematic **approach** to an overseas marketing strategy is beginning to take shape.

_____

_____

_____

m) The exchange rate is a significant **factor** in determining the volume of exports but is not normally a **factor** in trade with countries with fixed exchange rates.

_____

_____

_____

n) However, a rise in the value of the euro will be of great **benefit** to British exporters.

_____

_____

_____

o) We always try to get maximum **benefit** from the current economic situation.

_____

_____

_____

p) However, the **issue** of government over-regulation remains a problem for smaller companies.

_____

_____

_____

q) For example, the government has adopted a **policy** of requiring all businesses to submit certain documentation in advance.

_____

_____

_____

r) Government **policy** on such issues will increase running costs for small businesses.

_____

_____

_____

Language note: "Noun + noun" combinations are also called _compound nouns_.

7.2 Use the words in the box to make "noun + noun" combinations with the words in a) to c) below. You can place words from the box either before or after the words in a) to c).

> analysis   collection   decision-making   decisions   findings
> food   government   makers   production   team

Example:

policy   _government, makers, decisions, etc._

a) research   _____

b) data   _____

c) process   _____

7.3 Check in your dictionary to find nouns that can be used in combination with the nouns in a) to d) (either before or after).

Example:

source   _energy, light, power_

a) labour   _____

b) benefit   _____

c) export   _____

d) area   _____

Transitive or intransitive verbs

In earlier exercises in this unit we have seen examples of the following verbs which show that they can be used with noun phrases as objects: _analyse_, _define_, _establish_, _estimate_, _identify_, _assess_. All of these verbs are therefore transitive.

Examples:

- _Scientists are attempting to **assess** what <u>side-effects the drug may have</u>._
- _After years of research, scientists have **identified** <u>the cause of the disease</u>._

> **Language note:** Most dictionaries label transitive verbs as VT and intransitive verbs as VI.

7.4 The table below shows some other verbs from the AWL Sublist 1 that are always transitive and others which are always intransitive. Complete the table by putting the verbs in the box in the correct column.

> finance   function   involve   issue   legislate   occur   process

Transitive verbs		Intransitive verbs	
assume		proceed	
create			
distribute			

7.5   Copy an example sentence from your dictionary for each of the transitive verbs from the completed table in Excercise 7.4.

Example:

distribute: Aid agencies **are distributing** food and blankets to the victims of the earthquake.

_____

_____

_____

_____

_____

_____

_____

_____

_____

_____

_____

_____

_____

_____

7.6   Copy an example sentence from your dictionary for each of the intransitive verbs from the completed table in Exercise 7.4.

Example:

function: The airport is now **functioning** normally again.

_____

_____

_____

_____

_____

_____

_____

_____

_____

_____

_____

_____

_____

Language note: The meaning of a verb can change if it is used transitively or intransitively.

Verbs that are both transitive and intransitive

The following verbs are sometimes transitive and sometimes intransitive: *approach, benefit, research, vary, respond, interpret, indicate.*

7.7 Look at the verbs as they are used in these sentences and decide if they are transitive (VT) or intransitive (VI).

Example:

The drug will **benefit** a large number of patients. (_VT_)

a) This particular infection often fails to **respond** to antibiotics. (__)

b) The study **indicates** a strong connection between drug use and crime. (__)

c) They spoke good German, and promised to **interpret** for me. (__)

d) Waiting times **vary** and may be up to two months. (__)

e) It is important to **research** an overseas market carefully before setting up a sales operation. (__)

f) As winter **approaches**, many householders are storing fuel. (__)

7.8 Complete the sentences below with verbs from the box. Make a note after each sentence whether the verb is transitive (VT) or intransitive (VI).

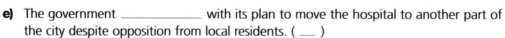

> ~~estimate~~   include   to establish   define   is proceeding   involving
>   have identified   require   indicates   varies

Example:

Health experts ___ _estimate_ ___ that regular exercise can increase life expectancy by around five percent. (_VT_)

Health

a) Visitors to the country no longer _____ a vaccination certificate. (__)

b) Treatment _____ according to the seriousness of the condition. (__)

c) Research _____ that over 81 percent of medical practitioners are dissatisfied with their salary. (__)

d) Doctors _____ a good patient as one who accepts their statements and their actions without question. (__)

e) The government _____ with its plan to move the hospital to another part of the city despite opposition from local residents. (__)

f) Scientists believe they _____ the gene that causes this hereditary condition. (__)

g) The purpose of the questionnaire was _____ whether smokers are more likely to lead sedentary lives. (__)

h) Patient assessment in this area of treatment will normally _____ a structured interview and a short questionnaire. (__)

i) The hospital has improved its working practices by _____ all staff in the decision-making process. (__)

Task 8: Review time

It is important you find time to review the exercises you have done in this unit and to review what you have learnt.

8.1 Look back through this unit and find:

a) five "noun + noun" collocations;

b) five nouns often followed by prepositions;

c) five words that can be either nouns or verbs.

8.2 Look back over all the exercises you have done and write down phrases that you think are useful and that you want to remember.

Examples:

… the most obvious drawback …
… according to one source …
… there is no reason to assume …
… it is clear that …
… according to the latest figures …
… can be interpreted …
… research suggests that …

Write your own notes and phrases here.

_____

_____

_____

_____

_____

_____

_____

_____

_____

_____

_____

_____

_____

_____

_____

_____

_____

_____

_____

_____

_____

_____

_____

8.3 Look at AWL Sublist 1 at the back of this book. Check if there are any words that you have not met in this unit and that you still do not know. Check the words in your dictionary and make notes on the meaning and how to use the word.

Example:

Word (word class)	Meanings
constitutional (adj)	• officially allowed or limited by the system of rules of a country or organisation
	• connected with the constitution of a country or organisation

Example phrases:

a constitutional right to privacy

a constitutional monarchy (i.e., a country ruled by a king or queen whose power is limited by a constitution)

a constitutional crisis

a constitutional reform / change / amendment

Other related words:

constitution (noun)

Your notes on other words:

_____

_____

_____

_____

_____

_____

_____

_____

_____

_____

_____

_____

_____

_____

_____

_____

_____

_____

_____

_____

_____

_____

_____

Vocabulary List

Business and Finance
business community
bank account
customer
economic
economical
economy
euro
exchange rate
export
financial
fraud
globalisation
inflation
labour
localisation
market change
marketing strategy
over-regulation
profit
risk
running costs
share trading
stock market
third quarter
uneconomical
value
wealth

Education
academic achievement
educationalist
higher education
historian
historical
physical education
school administrator
selection
streaming
study (n)

Environment
climate
emission
environmental issue
greenhouse gas
hydrological cycle
ozone layer

Health
AIDS
antibiotic
diet
disease
epidemic

gene
hereditary
infection
medical practitioner
medical researcher
physician
sedentary life
side-effect
symptom
treatment
vaccination certificate
virus

Research
consumer
finding
interview
questionnaire
random sample
statistics

Society
behaviour
class
constitutional monarchy
crime
human development
industrialised
infancy
life expectancy
policy
regional
resident
social factors

Verbs
accept
acquire
address
adopt
affect
allow
analyse
assess
assume (reasonably ~)
carry out (research)
consist (of)
continue (to be)
contract
date (from)
deal (with)
define
depend (on)
derive
establish

estimate
finance
function
gain
identify
ignore
indicate
inform
interpret
invest
involve
issue
legislate
occur
proceed
process
provide
raise
reduce
relocate
require
research
respond
solve
stem (from)
store
submit
suffer (from)
suggest
take place
take shape
treat
vary

Other
accurate
amendment
aspect
assessment
assumption
authority/ies
average
benefit
category
concept
consistent
controversial
creation
creative
crisis
data
decision-making process
detailed analysis
documentation
drawback

effect (n)
effective
estimate
evident
external control
factor
focus
formula
freely available
function (n)
fundamental
increase (n)
indication
indicative
individual
influence (n)
institution
interpretation
leading
limited
minority
officially
opposition
organisation
performance
point of view
popularity
practice (n)
project (n)
proposed cost
radical approach
rate
reduction
reform (n)
relationship
relatively
requirement
resources
response
responsive
right (n)
scientific evidence
sector
significant
source
specific
statement
supporting
systematic
technique
theory
variable
well-documented

7 AWL – Sublist 2

This unit will help you:
- familiarise yourself with the word families in AWL Sublist 2;
- practise understanding and using these words in context.

Task 1: Meanings of words

1.1 Study the words in bold in the extracts below and then do the matching exercise that follows.

Health

a) People can be given special exercise routines that are **appropriate** for their needs.

b) It is wrong to **equate** weight loss solely with diet.

c) Physical exercise can **affect** one's health in a number of positive ways.

d) For a healthy diet it is important to **restrict** the amount of fat consumed.

e) Swimming and weight training are quite **distinct** forms of exercise.

Environment

f) Many companies are now hoping to exploit the **potential** of the Arctic region.

g) In contrast to weather, climate is generally influenced by slow changes in **features** like the ocean, the land, the orbit of the Earth about the Sun, and the energy output of the Sun.

h) There is a **complex** relationship between climate change and weather patterns.

i) The drought and **consequent** famine affected large parts of the country.

j) Global warming is not the result of one single **aspect** of human behaviour.

Match the words on the left with the definitions on the right.

Example:

Word	**Meaning**
affect	to change or influence someone or something

Word	**Meaning**
affect	to ensure something stays within a limit or limits
appropriate	made up of multiple parts and often complicated
equate	the natural outcome that follows from a specific situation
distinct	a part of something that stands out as being important or interesting
potential	to change or influence someone or something
feature	the possibilities that something or someone has to offer
restrict	one of many parts of an idea or situation
aspect	to treat two things as equal or the same
complex	right for a specific use
consequent	obviously different or part of a contradictory type

Study tip: The difference between *effect* (n, v) and *affect* (v) is a common problem in English. Check with a dictionary if you are unclear about the difference.

1.2 Complete the pairs of sentences below with the words from Exercise 1.1. In each pair you need the same word for both sentences. In the case of verbs, a different ending may be needed for the word, e.g., ~s, ~ed, ~ing. In the case of nouns you have to decide whether the singular or plural form is appropriate.

Example:

Emergency aid will be sent to the areas most ___affected___ by the flooding.

Extreme weather ___affects___ many of the world's poorest regions.

a) The developmental needs of the new EU countries are quite _____ from those of the original member states.

The European Union consists of 25 countries with _____ cultural, linguistic and economic roots.

b) Federalism is a key _____ of American politics.

One _____ of the American system is the amount of autonomy each state has.

c) Few people understand the _____ issues of genetic engineering.

The processes involved in cloning are very _____.

d) Western behaviour is not regarded as _____ in many parts of the world.

In some countries people consider death to be the _____ punishment for possessing drugs.

e) The largest factory in the town was closed down and the _____ loss of jobs had a severe effect on the whole area.

Many people in the area are now unemployed and the _____ social problems are putting a strain on local resources.

f) In politics some people seem to _____ openness with aggression.

You simply can't _____ the policies of the main political parties with progressive environmental policies.

g) Many countries have _____ smoking in public places such as bars and restaurants.

Smoking is _____ to designated areas.

h) Developing countries need to maximise their _____ for economic growth.

Fair-trade initiatives have great _____ for creating new jobs in developing countries.

i) This book deals with the social and religious _____ of the society of the ancient Incas.

All _____ of Incan life were heavily influenced by religion.

Task 2: Multi-meaning words

2.1 The words in the box below have at least two meanings. Look at how they are used in the sentences that follow and choose the correct meaning.

> **aspect**   **community**   **conduct**   **consume**   **credit**   **element**
>   **feature**   **maintain**   **primary**   **range**

Example:

In 1991, John Stevens sent Anne to New York as a **feature** writer for one of his magazines.

a) a part of someone's face, such as their eyes, nose

b) a part of something that stands out as being important or interesting

c) an article given special prominence in a newspaper or a magazine

Answer: *c) an article given special prominence in a newspaper or a magazine*

1 However, she is rarely given any **credit** for all the hard work she does.
   a) an agreement with a company where a product is taken by a customer and paid for later
   b) appreciation or respect someone gets when they have done something well
   c) recognition a student gets from a college or university for completing a course

2 Developed countries **consume** huge quantities of raw materials.
   a) to make use of a quantity of something
   b) to eat or drink something
   c) to make something so that it can no longer be used

3 This is aggravated by the **range** of products demanded by the retail market.
   a) a set of items or people that are distinct but related
   b) the extent within which quantities of something vary
   c) the group of products that an organisation offers

4 The **primary** objective of the new legislation is to raise standards.
   a) most important or fundamental
   b) the name given to the education of children between ages five and eleven
   c) medically, the beginning of growth or development

5 However, many teachers **maintain** that the latest changes will lead to a decline in educational standards.
   a) to allow something to continue as it had previously or at the same level
   b) to uphold a degree of action or motion
   c) to be certain that what you believe is correct

6 The police are **conducting** a thorough investigation into the affair.
   a) to carry out a specific project or task, particularly to find out information
   b) to transmit electricity or heat along or through something
   c) to take or show someone around somewhere

7 The main suspect's story may contain an **element** of truth, even if the police do not accept his argument as a whole.
   a) a substance consisting of only one type of atom
   b) one part of a complicated system
   c) an amount, usually small, of a quality or feeling

8 The government is trying to reintegrate mentally ill people into the **community**.
   a) society and the people in it
   b) an area and the people who live in it
   c) plants and animals that can be found together in a specific area

9 Health and safety **aspects** have to be considered when designing new buildings.
   a) one of many features of something
   b) the direction in which a window, room or front of a building faces
   c) how something or someone looks

Task 3: Word classes

3.1 Check the following words in a dictionary. Then complete the table with the word class they belong to, i.e., noun, verb, adjective or adverb. Some words belong in more than one class.

Word	Word class
conclude	*verb*
acquire	
community	
relevant	
potential	

Word	Word class
resource	
transfer	
focus	
previous	
secure	

3.2 Decide what word class would fill each gap in the following sentences. Write *v* (verb), *n* (noun) or *adj* (adjective) in the brackets after each gap.

Example:

The newly elected president quickly reversed a lot of the policy decisions made by the _____ (adj) president.

Environment

a) Compared with the _____ (__) year, 50 percent more has been spent on environmental research.

b) The study _____ (__) that sea temperatures were rising by 1°C every nine years.

c) Experts are attempting to identify _____ (__) risks to coastal areas from flooding caused by melting ice in polar regions.

d) Many of the world's mineral _____ (__) have already been exhausted.

Politics

e) The _____ (__) of power to a civilian government took longer than expected.

f) The government says that these arguments are no longer _____ (__) in the new situation.

g) Many people do not feel _____ (__) as a result of the sharp rise in crime.

h) The government is attempting to _____ (__) new powers to deal with violent crime.

i) Good communications between central government and the local _____ (__) will be essential.

3.3 Complete the sentences in Exercise 3.2 with words from the box in Exercise 3.1. In the case of verbs, a different ending may be needed for the word, e.g., ~s, ~ed, ~ing. In the case of nouns you have to decide whether the singular or plural form is appropriate.

Example:

The newly elected president quickly reversed a lot of the policy decisions made by the ___previous___ (adj) president.

Task 4: Word families

Look at these two sentences.

- *Some $15 billion was **invested** in the former Soviet bloc in Europe and Central Asia.*

- *Even North Korea, facing severe food shortages and economic decline, is keen to attract foreign **investment**.*

The highlighted words, *invested* (verb) and *investment* (noun), are both members of the same word family. The word *invested* can also be used as an adjective, but in this word family there is no adverb.

4.1 Put the words in the box below into the table with other members of their families. Remember that you may not be able to complete every column for each word, but there may be some columns where there are two entries. For example, *participation* and *participant* are both nouns.

> achievement selective complexity normality distinction maintenance computerise
> perceive regulation participant resourceful participation strategic regional

Nouns	Verbs	Adjectives	Adverbs
achievement	achieve		
		normal	
	participate		
	maintain		
perception			
	regulate		
strategy			
	select		
region			
resource			
		complex	
		distinct	
computer			

4.2 Choose the correct form of the word in brackets to complete the following sentences. In the case of verbs, a different ending may be needed for the word, e.g., ~s, ~ed, ~ing. In the case of nouns you have to decide whether the singular or plural form is appropriate.

Example:

Some medical experts do not make any ___distinction___ between the two conditions. (distinct)

Health

a) Contrary to popular _____, vigorous exercise is not necessarily good for your health. (perceive)

b) The _____ of medical practitioners in the decision-making process is absolutely essential. (participate)

c) The discovery of penicillin was one of the major medical _____ of the 20th century. (achieve)

d) A new _____ is needed to tackle the growing problem of AIDS in Africa. (strategy)

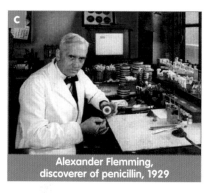
Alexander Flemming, discoverer of penicillin, 1929

Economics

e) Many believe that higher inflation is a direct _____ of the increase in the price of oil. (consequent)

f) The _____ of a stable and low rate of inflation is essential for economic development. (maintain)

g) The economy should be allowed to develop independently without the _____ of artificial government measures. (assist)

h) The government is often highly _____ in assigning funds to economically disadvantaged regions. (select)

i) Financial _____ in this sector are very strict. (regulate)

Task 5: Prefixes

The following prefixes are used with a number of the words from AWL Sublist 2.

Prefix	Meaning
re~	again
in~, un~, ab~, ir~	not, the opposite of
under~	not enough

5.1 Which of the above prefixes can be used with the following words?

Example:

secure   _insecure_

a) relevant   _____

b) regulated   _____

c) appropriate   _____

d) construct   _____

e) affected   _____

f) normal   _____

g) invest   _____

h) obtainable   _____

i) restricted   _____

j) conclusive   _____

5.2 Complete the following sentences using either:

• the word in brackets; or

• a prefix + the word in brackets.

In the case of verbs you should choose the correct ending, e.g., ~ed, ~ing, ~s. In the case of nouns you have to decide whether the singular or plural form is appropriate.

Example:

An incorrect diagnosis of the patient's illness resulted in him receiving completely _inappropriate_ treatment. (appropriate)

Health

a) _____ information can often delay an accurate diagnosis of a patient's condition. (relevant)

b) Many hospitals are now allowing completely _____ access to people visiting patients. (restricted)

c) Measurement of a body temperature of 40°C (104°F) indicates the presence of some _____ condition or symptom. (normal)

d) The patient received serious injuries in the accident but her vital organs were _____ . (affected)

Business and Finance

e) The _____ of the buildings was funded by bank loans. (construction)

f) Make sure an investment broker is officially _____ and authorised before you hand over any of your money. (regulated)

g) Investment funds usually _____ their profits rather than pay them out to shareholders. (invest)

h) Zero inflation is an unrealistic and _____ goal for the economy at this stage in its development. (obtainable)

i) The results of the investigation were _____ so the company's accounts will have to be examined again. (conclusive)

Task 6: Collocations

Verbs and nouns

Look at these "verb + noun" combinations that appear in this unit.

- *(re)invest profits*
- *restrict access*

6.1 Match the verbs on the left with the nouns on the right to make combinations that can all be found in the previous exercises in this unit.

Example:

exploit the potential of globalisation (Exercise 1.1, sentence f)

Verb	Noun
exploit	investment
make	an investigation
affect	the potential of something
attract	a distinction
conduct	access
restrict	one's health

6.2 Choose one verb from the box that fits best with all the nouns in each group.

| ~~achieve~~ | affect | consume | design | evaluate | maintain | perceive | transfer |

Example:

	achieve	good results, objectives, high standards, success
a)	_____	productivity, business, development, rates
b)	_____	standards, quality, the status quo, interest
c)	_____	needs, problems, threats, differences
d)	_____	food, time, quantities, goods
e)	_____	clothes, buildings, systems, courses
f)	_____	money, funds, accounts, data
g)	_____	effects, alternatives, effectiveness, evidence

Adjectives and nouns

6.3 Choose one adjective from the box that fits best with all the nouns in each group.

| appropriate | ~~complex~~ | final | normal | positive | primary |

Example:

	complex	problem, relationship, structure
a)	_____	objective, aim, function, purpose, concern, importance
b)	_____	response, effect, influence, aspect, impact, experience
c)	_____	decision, analysis, outcome, product, result, stage
d)	_____	circumstances, practice, life, distribution, conditions
e)	_____	action, time, response, manner, choice

Discovering collocations

You will learn a lot of collocations by paying attention to the way words are used in texts.

6.4 Look at the words in bold in the following sentences. Identify different combinations of verbs, nouns, adjectives and adverbs. Then answer the questions that follow.

a) Technological advances are affecting every **aspect** of life.

b) We need to focus on the economic and social **aspects** of the problem.

c) Changes in energy policy will have a huge **impact** on the environment.

d) Experts are trying to reduce the **impact** of the oil spill on marine life.

e) Internet companies offer a vast **range** of products.

f) Software companies can provide a wide **range** of solutions.

g) We can't make a decision until we have all the **relevant** information.

h) The remaining information is particularly **relevant** to our work.

i) Volunteers were paid for their **participation** in the research.

j) The government is looking at ways of increasing voter **participation** in elections.

k) There is no standardised body for the **regulation** of money markets.

l) The effectiveness of the proposals depends on how the authorities decide to enforce the **regulations**.

m) The proposals make a **distinction** between companies registered in this country and those registered overseas.

n) The government decided to lift **restrictions** on the export of foreign currency.

o) No currency or exchange **restrictions** are imposed on registered companies.

p) The findings of the survey have far-reaching **consequences** for consumers.

q) Criminals usually have to face the **consequences** of their actions.

r) The **report** was commissioned by the government.

Questions:

a) What verbs are used with these nouns?

_____	impact
_____	regulations
_____	distinction
_____	restrictions
_____	consequences
_____	report

b) What nouns are used after these words?

aspect(s) of	_____
participation in	_____
relevant (to)	_____
regulation of	_____
range of	_____

c) What adjectives are used before these nouns?

_____	range
_____	impact
_____	aspect(s)
_____	consequences

d) What adverb is used before this word?

_____	relevant

Task 7: Word grammar

Discovering noun patterns

You have studied the following patterns in Unit 5: Word grammar. Exercise 7.1 will help you notice these patterns in the texts you read.

- noun + preposition, e.g., *distinction between*
- noun followed by *that*, e.g., *perception that*
- noun + noun, e.g., *population growth*

7.1 Look at the highlighted nouns in the sentences below and identify:

- what prepositions are used after the nouns;
- which nouns are followed by "*that* + clause";
- which "noun + noun" combinations are used.

Health

a) It is vital to understand the **distinction** between bacterial infections and viral infections.

_____

_____

_____

b) We need to assess the potential **impact** of avian flu on the human population.

_____

_____

_____

c) The **focus** of the conference shifted from population growth to the eradication of common diseases.

_____

_____

d) There is a widespread **perception** that antiviral drugs can be developed quickly.

_____

_____

_____

e) The **relevance** of this concept to physicians is discussed in theoretical terms in this chapter.

_____

_____

_____

f) The **restrictions** on importing drugs are designed to limit the potential **impact** of unlicensed drugs on the local market.

_____

_____

_____

Sport

g) The test measures children's **achievements** in different sports.

_____

_____

_____

h) The sporting **achievements** of the team captain have been recorded in a new book.

_____

_____

_____

i) Active **participation** in sporting activities is a requirement for most young children.

_____

_____

_____

j) The emphasis is on **participation** by teenagers and young adults in local projects.

_____

_____

_____

k) The **emphasis** is on the success of the team rather than on the **achievement** of individual players.

_____

_____

_____

Environment

l) The **acquisition** of the company is being investigated by the Monopolies Commission.

_____

_____

_____

m) If sea levels continue to rise, it will have very serious **consequences** for many cities in low-lying areas.

_____

_____

_____

n) More extreme weather conditions are the unavoidable **consequences** of global warming.

_____

_____

_____

"Noun + noun" combinations

Here are some more examples of "noun + noun" combinations from Exercise 6.4.

- *money markets* (sentence k)
- *exchange restrictions* (sentence o)

7.2 Use the words in the box to make "noun + noun" combinations with the words in a) to c) below. You can place words from the box either before or after the words in a) to c).

> ~~consumption~~   computer   construction   restrictions

Example:

    energy, food, fuel, alcohol   *consumption*

a) system, screen, software, programmer, industry   _____

b) manager, industry, work, company   _____

c) speed, trade, travel, import   _____

7.3 Check in your dictionary and find nouns that can be used in combination with the following nouns in a) to c) (either before or after).

Example:

    review   *marketing, corporate, business, development, strategy*

a) regulations   _____

b) security   _____

c) administrators   _____

> **Study tip:** For more information about noun patterns, see Unit 4: Collocations.

Transitive or intransitive verbs

In earlier exercises in this unit we have seen examples of the following verbs which show that they can be used with noun phrases as objects: *affect, achieve, acquire, conduct, construct, consume, invest, maintain, restrict*. All of these verbs are therefore transitive.

Example:

- *Environmental factors can **affect** human development before birth.*

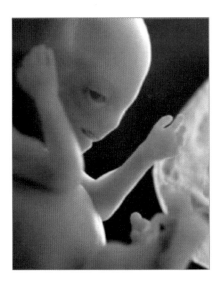

7.4 The table below shows some other verbs from the AWL Sublist 2 that are always transitive and others that are always intransitive. Complete the table by putting the verbs in the box in the correct column.

| credit | reside | feature | finalise | regulate | secure | perceive | select | survey |

Transitive verbs		Intransitive verbs	
categorise		participate	
equate			
evaluate			
design			
injure			
purchase			
seek			

Study tip: See Unit 5: Word grammar for more on transitive and intransitive verbs.

7.5 Copy an example sentence from your dictionary for each of the transitive verbs from the completed table in Exercise 7.4.

Example:

categorise: The population is categorised according to age, sex and social group.

7.6 Copy an example sentence from your dictionary for each of the intransitive verbs from the completed table in Exercise 7.4.

Example:

participate: Everyone in the class is expected to **participate** actively in these discussions.

_____

_____

_____

_____

_____

_____

_____

_____

_____

_____

_____

_____

_____

_____

Language note: Verbs sometimes have different meanings when used transitively or intransitively.

Verbs that are both transitive and intransitive

The following verbs are sometimes transitive and sometimes intransitive: *assist, conclude, focus, transfer, obtain, impact.*

7.7 Look at the verbs as they are used in these sentences and decide if they are transitive (VT) or intransitive (VI).

Example:

This leaflet will **assist** consumers in selecting the best insurance policy. (VT)

a) The report **concludes** with references to the rise in inflation and the decline in business optimism. (___)

b) Ideas that work well in one situation may not **transfer** well to another. (___)

c) The research project will **focus** on social problems in the city. (___)

d) The purpose of the research is to identify problem areas and to **obtain** objective data for analysis. (___)

e) The new law will progressively **impact** on the way businesses operate. (___)

Task 8: Review time

It is important you find time to review the exercises you have done in this unit and to review what you have learnt.

8.1 Look back through the unit and find:

a) five "adjective + noun" collocations;

b) five "noun + noun" collocations;

c) five nouns often followed by prepositions;

d) five words that can be either nouns or verbs.

8.2 Look back over all the exercises you have done and write down phrases that you think are useful and that you want to remember.

Examples:

… it is wrong to equate …

… in contrast to …

… the primary objective of …

… conduct a thorough investigation into …

… may contain an element of truth …

… compared with the previous year …

… make a distinction between …

Write your own notes and phrases here.

8.3 Look at AWL Sublist 2 at the back of this book. Check if there are any words that you have not met in this unit and that you do not know. Check the words in your dictionary and make notes on the meaning and how to use the word.

Example notes:

Word (word class)	Meanings
item (noun)	• *a single thing, especially one thing in a list, group or set of things*
	• *a single, usually short, piece of news in a newspaper or magazine, or on television*

Example phrases:

an item of clothing / furniture / jewellery

an item on the agenda / list / menu

luxury items

a news item

Other related words:

itemise (transitive verb)

Your notes on other words:

_____

_____

_____

_____

_____

_____

_____

_____

_____

_____

_____

_____

_____

_____

_____

_____

_____

_____

_____

_____

_____

_____

_____

Vocabulary List

Business and Finance
acquisition
bank loan
business optimism
company accounts
corporate
credit
developed country
developing country
economic decline
development
economic growth
disadvantaged
exchange restriction
fair-trade initiative
financial regulation
foreign investment
funds
insurance policy
Internet company
investment broker
investment fund
money market
Monopolies Commission
productivity
raw materials
regulation
retail market
shareholder
software company
zero inflation

Education
educational standards

Environment
Arctic region
climate change
coastal area
developmental needs
drought
emergency aid
energy output
environmental policy
extreme weather
famine
flooding
global warming
low-lying area
marine life
mineral resources
oil spill
orbit
polar region
sea level
weather pattern

Health
avian flu
bacterial infection
body temperature
cloning
diagnosis
exercise routine
genetic engineering
health and safety
healthy diet
mentally ill
penicillin
physical exercise
vigorous exercise
viral infection
vital organ
weight loss
weight training

Politics
civilian government
election
European Union (EU)
federalism
legislation
member state
newly elected
policy decision
political party
Soviet bloc
voter participation

Research
objective data

Society
central government
community
government measure
local resources
population growth
public place
punishment
religious
social group
social problem
suspect (n)
investigation
unemployed
violent crime

Verbs
aggravate
assign
attempt
attract (investment)
categorise
commission
computerise
conduct
consume
destroy
equate
exhaust
exploit (the potential of)
express
finalise
hand over
impact
influence
injure
maintain
make (a distinction)
maximise
participate
perceive
possess
purchase
register
regulate
reintegrate
reside
restrict (access)
reverse
secure
survey
tackle

Other
according to
appropriate
argument
artificial
authorised
belief
chemical substance
circumstances
complexity
consequent
contrary to (popular opinion)
cultural
designated area
distinction
element of truth (an ~)
essential
far-reaching consequences
feature writer
impact
in contrast to
linguistic
maintenance
normality
participant
participation
potential impact
presence
primary objective
progressively
range
relevant information
resourceful
selective
severe effect
standardised
strain
strategic
theoretical
unavoidable consequences
volunteer (n)
widespread perception

8 AWL – Sublist 3

This unit will help you:
- familiarise yourself with the word families in AWL Sublist 3;
- practise understanding and using these words in context.

Task 1: Meanings of words

Study tip: As you do these exercises, pay special attention to the word class of each individual word.

1.1 Study the words in bold in the extracts below and then do the matching exercise that follows.

Manufacturing

a) The machine consists of more than two hundred different **components**.

b) It is fully guaranteed for a period of five years **excluding** electrical parts.

c) Its **initial** performance should match the criteria set out in the technical specifications.

d) Any operator mishandling of the machine may **constrain** the liability of the manufacturer to replace malfunctioning components.

e) The manufacturer retains the right to refuse **consent** for repair work to be carried out if the terms of the contract have been broken.

Science

f) Darwin's observations led him to **deduce** that animals could adapt to their surroundings.

g) The **dominant** male baboon is the largest in the group.

h) In certain groups of apes and other primates there is a **core** of animals which enjoy greater power than the other members of the group.

i) Ape society seems to consist of different **layers** of seniority.

j) At the moment it's impossible to say for sure what the **outcome** of the research will be.

Match the words on the left with the definitions on the right.

Example:

Word	Meaning
component	one of the different parts that a machine or system consists of

Word	Meaning
component	to produce an opinion as a result of information
excluding	stronger or more obvious than other people or things which are similar
core	to prevent something from happening
consent	the strongest members of a group
constrain	happening when something first starts
dominant	the result or consequences of something
initial	to allow something to happen
outcome	one of several levels within an organisation
layer	not including
deduce	one of the many parts that make up a machine or system

1.2 Complete the pairs of sentences below with the words from Exercise 1.1. In each pair you need the same word for both sentences. In the case of verbs, a different ending may be needed for the word, e.g., ~s, ~ed, ~ing. In the case of nouns you have to decide whether the singular or plural form is appropriate.

Example:

Semiconductors are the principal _components_ of many electronic circuits.

The factory makes car engine _components_ .

a) The negotiations are continuing, and everyone is hoping for a positive _____ .

The best _____ for all concerned would be an agreement bringing peace to the region.

b) The company is trying to maintain its _____ position in the market.

Ten years ago the company enjoyed a _____ share of the market.

c) Parental _____ is needed before medical procedures can be carried out on children.

Without the prior _____ of the patient, doctors are unable to proceed with the operation.

d) The course costs £900, _____ accommodation.

_____ insurance, the total cost of the holiday is £450.

e) The _____ stage of the project is to build the transport infrastructure.

After the _____ work has been completed, the main phase of the construction project will begin.

f) 15- to 20-year-olds are the radio station's _____ audience.

The company will need a new _____ of highly trained research personnel if it is to succeed.

g) A large hole in the ozone _____ has appeared over Antarctica.

The road was covered in a thick _____ of ice.

h) Carbon dating procedures enable scientists to _____ the probable age of ancient remains.

Scientists have found shellfish fossils and _____ that the area had once been covered by water.

i) Planning regulations _____ building development in the past.

Plans to build new medical facilities have been _____ by financial problems.

Task 2: Multi-meaning words

2.1   The words in the box below have at least two meanings. Look at how they are used in the sentences that follow and choose the correct meaning.

compensate	constant	contribute	core	correspond	deduction
demonstrate	fund	illustrate	imply	justify	register	shift	valid

Example:

The temperature at the Earth's **core** is believed to be between 3000 and 5000°C.

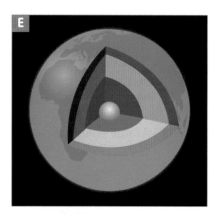

a) the hard central part of a fruit such as an apple that contains the seeds

b) the strongest, most supportive members of a group

c) the middle of a planet

Answer: *c) the middle of a planet*

1   A number of different human activities have **contributed** to climate change.

    a)   to add your money, goods, ideas or time and effort to something

    b)   to be one of the reasons that something happen

    c)   something that you have written for a newspaper or magazine

2   Frozen products containing milk fats must be stored at a **constant** temperature.

    a)   of a regular nature over a period of time

    b)   remaining at the same level or amount

    c)   loyal to a person or friend

3   The wording of the latest document closely **corresponds** to the existing law.

    a)   to be like something else or very similar to it

    b)   to exchange letters with someone regularly

    c)   to be related or linked with something else

4   The team's defence was very weak so the attackers had to work much harder to **compensate**.

    a)   to balance the effect of something negative

    b)   to pay someone money for an injury or loss

5   The studies clearly **demonstrate** the link between fossil fuels and climate change.

    a)   to show that something is true

    b)   to show another person how to do something by doing it yourself

    c)   to protest against or support something with a lot of other people in a public place

6 The ideas of the pioneers of aviation are as **valid** today as they were one hundred years ago.

  a) a valid ticket or document is acceptable, officially

  b) a valid argument is a reasonable one that most people would accept

  c) a valid user name or password will be accepted by a computer system

7 The discovery of metal implements **implies** that the ancient people of this region were able to produce things with iron.

  a) to suggest that something is likely to exist or to be true

  b) to suggest that you think something although you do not say it directly

8 There has been an enormous **shift** in attitudes towards smoking during the past 20 years.

  a) a change in something

  b) a period of work time in a factory

  c) a key on a computer keyboard

9 No matter how much provocation there is, violence of this kind can never be **justified**.

  a) to show there is a good explanation for something that other people may think is unreasonable

  b) to be an acceptable reason for something

  c) to make the left or right edges of a piece of writing straight

10 A **fund** has been set up to help the victims of the earthquake.

  a) a supply of money that people collect and keep for a specific reason

  b) a large amount of something which is usually useful

11 The history of the colonisation of Africa clearly **illustrates** the point.

  a) to explain something using pictures, diagrams and graphs to show your meaning

  b) to be an example which shows that something is correct or factual

  c) to put artwork in a book, magazine article, etc.

12 The earthquake **registered** 6.9 on the Richter Scale.

  a) to enter someone's name on an official list

  b) to give your opinion about something officially so that everyone knows your feelings

  c) to show as a measurement on a piece of equipment

13 Employees in this country pay up to 40 percent of their income in tax and other **deductions**.

  a) using evidence or information in order to understand something

  b) the amount that is subtracted from a total or the process of subtraction

Task 3: Word classes

3.1 Check the following words in a dictionary. Then complete the table with the word class they belong to, i.e., noun, verb, adjective or adverb. Some words belong in more than one class.

Word	Word class	Word	Word class
shift	noun, verb	consent	
link		minority	
proportion		register	
sequence		specify	
volume		comment	
alternative		emphasise	

3.2 Decide what word class would fill each gap in the following sentences. Write *v* (verb), *n* (noun) or *adj* (adjective) in the brackets after each gap.

Example:

The _____ (_n_) of Japanese imports has decreased noticeably over the past five years.

Science

a) Virtually all children go through the same _____ (__) of motor behaviours in the same order.

b) Scientists have _____ (__) environmental factors with the development of unborn babies.

c) The theory of evolution _____ (__) the biological basis of human development.

d) A high _____ (__) of babies born to mothers who were smokers have a less than average body weight at birth.

e) The book details _____ (__) ways to bring up young children.

Health

f) Patients have the right to refuse _____ (__) for a particular treatment at any time.

g) Journalists often ask doctors about the health of famous patients but they usually refuse to _____ (__).

h) Manufacturers of pharmaceuticals have to _____ (__) clearly which side effects patients might experience.

i) Employees from ethnic _____ (__) account for up to 40 percent of the total number of health workers in certain areas of the country.

j) All patients must be _____ (__) on arrival at the hospital.

k) Once again scientists are _____ (__) their focus back towards a virus as the most likely cause of the problem.

3.3 Now complete the sentences in Exercise 3.2 with words from the table in Exercise 3.1. In the case of verbs, a different ending may be needed for the word, e.g., ~s, ~ed, ~ing. In the case of nouns you have to decide whether the singular or plural form is appropriate.

Example:

The ____volume____ (n) of Japanese imports has decreased noticeably over the past five years.

Task 4: Word families

Look at these sentences.

> Many governments began trying to control **immigration**.

> The numbers of legal and illegal **immigrants** grew nonetheless, as economics had its way.

Source: Slaght, J., Harben, P., Pallant, A. (2006). *English for Academic Study: Reading and Writing Source Book*. Reading: Garnet Education.

The highlighted words, *immigration* and *immigrants*, are both members of the same word family and the writer uses them to make the writing more cohesive.

4.1 Put the words in the box below into the table with other members of their families. Remember that you may not be able to complete every column for each word, but there may be some columns where there are two entries.

> ~~reaction~~   exclusively   alternatively   exclusively   compensation   constantly
> locate   constraint   proportional   contribution   validity   justification   specific
> correspondingly   sufficiently   deduction   reliable   emphasise   illustrate
> reliability   exclusively   initially   reliance

Nouns	Verbs	Adjectives	Adverbs
reaction	react		
validation			
	specify		
	rely		
illustration			
location			

Nouns	Verbs	Adjectives	Adverbs
	justify		
	imply		
		initial	
	correspond		
		alternative	
	compensate		
	contribute		
		constant	
	constrain		
	deduce		
		exclusive	
proportion			
		sufficient	
emphasis			

4.2   Choose the correct form of the word in brackets to complete the following sentences. In the case of verbs a different ending may be needed for the word, e.g., ~ed, ~ing, ~s. In the case of nouns you have to decide whether the singular or plural form is more appropriate.

Example:

The government will pay full ___compensation___ to businesses affected by the new regulation. (compensate)

Business and Finance

a)   The company has decided to place greater _____ on developing new products. (emphasise)

b)   _____, we had planned to focus solely on the domestic market. (initial)

c)   However, the favourable _____ of many overseas customers to our latest range forced us to change our strategy. (react)

d)   Focusing on research and development will have _____ for short-term profitability. (imply)

e)   Our task will be to develop _____ products that will be successful in key markets. (specify)

f)   We will need to ensure that these products are _____ geared to the demands of those markets. (sufficient)

g)   We are _____ reviewing our export strategy. (constant)

h)   We could concentrate on existing markets or, _____, we could try to break into new ones. (alternative)

i)   The management team is confident that the new strategy will make a positive _____ to the future of the company. (contribute)

Task 5: Prefixes

The following prefixes are used with a number of the words from the AWL Sublist 3.

Prefix	Meaning
re~	again
in~, un~, dis~, de~	not, the opposite of

5.1   Which of the above prefixes can be used with the following words?

Example:

     validate   ___invalidate___

a)   sufficient   _____

b)   specified   _____

c)   reliable   _____

d)   proportionate   _____

e)   locate   _____

f)   justified   _____

g)   conventional   _____

5.2 Complete the following sentences using either:

- the word in brackets; or

- a prefix + the word in brackets.

In the case of verbs you should choose the correct ending, e.g., ~ed, ~ing, ~s.

Example:

His behaviour has often been regarded as unusual and _unconventional_ and he has been criticised by many of his colleagues. (conventional)

Research

a) Statistics can sometimes be _____ and lead to over-generalised conclusions. (reliable)

b) The conclusions of the report are _____ by the low number of people in the survey. (validate)

c) If the amount of data available is _____ the study cannot be conducted properly. (sufficient)

d) The high level of crime in the city has forced the company to _____ to a rural area. (locate)

e) The study reveals that 80 percent of complaints were _____ and a waste of police time. (justify)

Task 6: Collocations

Verbs and nouns

Look at these "verb + noun" combinations that appear in this unit.

- *invalidate a conclusion*

- *refuse consent*

- *pay compensation*

6.1 Complete the sentences below using one of the verbs in the box. Pay particular attention to the bold noun in each sentence and find a verb that collocates with that noun. You will need to use each verb once only.

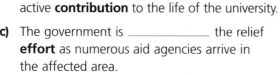

> **be   coordinate   demonstrate   follow   give   justify**
> **make   maximise   ~~meet~~   pay   predict**

Example:

All applicants must ____meet____ the entry **criteria** for this course.

a) They must also _____ a **commitment** to this highly specialised field of study.

b) Students are expected to _____ an active **contribution** to the life of the university.

c) The government is _____ the relief **effort** as numerous aid agencies arrive in the affected area.

d) They have already agreed to _____ **compensation** to the victims of the disaster.

e) The Ministry of Finance has _____ its **consent** to the release of more funds to help the victims.

f) With both parties level in the opinion polls, it is very difficult to _____ the **outcome** of the election.

g) There _____ a big **shift** in public opinion since the last election.

h) Some government ministers have made mistakes and have had to _____ their **actions** in parliament.

i) The main focus of the company is to _____ a **profit** this year and that will require some risk-taking.

j) The numbers _____ a logical **sequence**.

6.2 Choose one verb from the box that fits best with all the nouns in each group.

~~justify~~   shift   emphasise   dominate   illustrate   exclude

Example:

___justify___	action, argument, cost, position
a) _____	a point, a need, importance, value
b) _____	funds, attention, responsibility, power
c) _____	the world, the market, the industry, the news
d) _____	the point, the difficulty, problem, importance
e) _____	people, children, evidence, possibility

6.3 Complete the sentences below with an appropriate "verb + noun" combination from Exercise 6.2. The first letter of each noun is given to help you. Pay attention to the form and tense of the verb in each sentence.

Example:

___Children___ who are ___excluded___ from school often end up wandering the streets.

a) I am going to _____ this p_____ by showing you a diagram.

b) The report _____ the i_____ of implementing safety standards.

c) Men still tend to _____ the w_____ of professional sport – there are hardly any women involved in football management, for example.

d) The government hopes the latest good news from overseas will _____ the media's a_____ away from the current economic problems.

Adjectives and nouns

6.4 Match the adjectives on the left with the nouns on the right to make combinations that can all be found in the previous exercises in this unit.

Examples:

initial stage (Exercise 1.2, sentence e)

Adjective	Noun
initial	position
ethnic	ideas
positive	temperature
dominant	compensation
constant	minorities
different	stage
alternative	outcome
valid	components
full	shift
enormous	ways of coping

6.5 Which nouns are commonly used with these adjectives? Find some matching nouns in your dictionary.

Example:

    initial   *reaction, impression, etc.* _____

a) sufficient   _____

b) specific   _____

c) valid   _____

d) reliable   _____

e) minor   _____

Discovering collocations

You will learn a lot of collocations by paying attention to the way words are used in texts.

6.6 Look at the words in bold in the following sentences. Identify different combinations of verbs, nouns, adjectives and prepositions. Then answer the questions that follow.

a) The disposal of non-recyclable items can have serious **implications** for the environment.

b) The plan to build a new waste disposal plant was abandoned because of the potential social and environmental **implications**.

c) Payment of the full amount can be delayed under certain **circumstances**.

d) In exceptional **circumstances** a refund may be considered.

e) Toxicity is not the only **criterion** for classifying a drug as dangerous.

f) The government is drawing up new **criteria** for the classification of drugs and other harmful substances.

g) This proposal provides a **framework** for future discussion.

h) The purpose of this meeting is to draw up a simple **framework** with which we can move forward.

i) This disease affects a significant **proportion** of the population.

j) Although the majority of sufferers are women, a small **proportion** – about five percent – are men.

k) The Ministry has proposed a **scheme** to make more use of wind and tidal energy.

l) Under a new government **scheme**, householders are being encouraged to switch to solar energy.

m) Troops have been sent to the region in **reaction** to the riots.

n) When the trouble broke out the government's first **reaction** was to deny that it was their responsibility.

o) Most people are willing to allow their names to be used for publicity if this is done with their prior **consent**.

p) Photographs may not be taken without the subject's **consent**.

q) Voluntary workers make a huge **contribution** to society.

r) The university has made a significant **contribution** to the economic regeneration of the city.

Questions

Example:

a) What verbs control these nouns?

provide	a framework
_____	implications
_____	criteria
_____	contribution

b) What adjectives are used before these nouns?

_____	implications
_____	circumstances
_____	criterion
_____	proportion
_____	reaction
_____	consent
_____	contribution

c) What prepositions are used after these nouns?

criterion/criteria   _____

framework   _____

proportion   _____

reaction   _____

d) What prepositions are used before these nouns?

_____   circumstances

_____   consent

Study tip: Although the Academic Word Lists may appear long, you will find that you already recognise many of the words. The more you work with words the more you will deepen your understanding of vocabulary.

Task 7: Word grammar

Discovering noun patterns

You have studied the following patterns in Unit 5: Word grammar. Exercise 7.1 will help you notice these patterns in the texts you read.

- noun + preposition, e.g., *alternative to*
- noun followed by *that*, e.g., *implication that*
- noun + noun, e.g., *health aspects*
- noun followed by *to be*, e.g., *the alternative is*

7.1 Look at the highlighted nouns in the sentences below and identify:

- what prepositions are used after the nouns;
- which nouns are followed by "*that* + clause";
- what prepositions come before *core* and *instance*;
- which noun is followed by "*to* + infinitive";
- which nouns are followed by the verb *to be* (i.e., *is*, *are*, etc.) + *to* + infinitive.

Health

a) This particular treatment is offered as an **alternative** to invasive surgery.

_____

_____

_____

b) The **alternative** is to operate on the patient immediately and this might cause complications.

_____

_____

_____

c) Applications from non-smokers were encouraged, with the **implication** that smokers would not be considered for the position.

No Smoking in the Bar

Thank You

d) This new legislation banning smoking in pubs and restaurants has profound **implications** for social life in the UK.

e) The research examines the **implications** of the experiences of Ireland and Norway in prohibiting smoking in all public places.

f) The legislation lays particular **emphasis** on the health aspects of passive smoking.

g) A significant **proportion** of young people start smoking in their early teens.

h) Peer pressure is at the **core** of the problem.

i) Researchers have also come across many **instances** of health problems relating to poor diet.

Environment

j) The continuing lack of rainfall is having a serious impact on the **volume** of water in the reservoir.

_____

_____

_____

k) There are various **techniques** for dealing with industrial pollution.

_____

_____

_____

l) The authorities are examining a number of **schemes** to pump water into the reservoir from nearby rivers.

_____

_____

_____

m) However, the **reaction** to these plans has not been positive.

_____

_____

_____

n) Conservationists are calling for alternative **techniques** of water conservation to be applied in this particular case.

_____

_____

_____

o) In this particular **instance**, the authorities admit they may have made an error of judgement.

_____

_____

_____

"Noun + noun" combinations

Here are some more examples of "noun + noun" combinations from previous exercises in this unit.

- _fossil fuel_ (Exercise 2.1, sentence 6)
- _government scheme_ (Exercise 6.6, sentence l)

7.2 Match nouns from the left and right columns to make "noun + noun" combinations that can be found in the preceding exercises in this unit.

Example:

management team

Noun 1	Noun 2
management	change
ozone	team
climate	layer
repair	station
car	pressure
radio	work
metal	infrastructure
stock	exchange
peer	engine
transport	implements

> **Study tip:** For more information about noun patterns, see Unit 4: Collocations.

Transitive or intransitive verbs

In earlier exercises in this unit we have seen examples of the following verbs which show that they can be used with noun phrases as objects: *constrain, coordinate, demonstrate, illustrate, justify, link, shift, invalidate, maximise, emphasise, dominate, exclude*. All of these verbs are transitive.

Examples:

● *Children who are **excluded** from school often end up wandering the streets.*

7.3 The table below shows some other verbs from the AWL Sublist 3 which are always transitive and others which are always intransitive. Complete the table below by putting the verbs in the box in the correct column.

correspond	deduce	ensure	imply	interact

Transitive verbs		Intransitive verbs	
fund	specify	consent	
negate			
publish			
remove			

7.4 Copy an example sentence from your dictionary for each of the transitive verbs from the completed table in Exercise 7.3.

Example:

fund: Many people believe that the insurgents **are being funded** from abroad.

7.5 Copy an example sentence from your dictionary for each of the intransitive verbs from the completed table in Exercise 7.3.

Example:

consent: After a long delay they finally **consented to** the construction of the new motorway.

Language note: Verbs sometimes have different meanings when used transitively or intransitively.

Verbs that are both transitive and intransitive

The following verbs are sometimes transitive and sometimes intransitive: *compensate, contribute, convene, register.*

7.6 Look at the verbs as they are used in these sentences and decide if they are transitive (VT) or intransitive (VI).

a) My parents said they would **contribute** something towards the cost of my driving lessons. (___)

b) His enthusiasm **compensates** for his lack of experience. (___)

c) The Parliament will next **convene** on October 4. (___)

d) Owners had until the end of 1990 to **register** their weapons. (___)

e) Large retail chains are usually only prepared to **locate** stores in areas of high population density. (___)

Verbs followed by "(*that*) + clause"

In earlier exercises you will have seen that some verbs can be followed by "(*that*) + clause", for example, in Exercise 1.1:

● *Darwin's observations led him to **deduce** that animals could adapt to their surroundings.*

… and in Exercise 2.1:

● *The discovery of metal implements **implies** that the ancient people of this region were able to smelt iron.*

7.7 Check in your dictionary and circle the words in the box that can be used with "(*that*) + clause". Copy example sentences from your dictionary.

⟨comment⟩ dominate emphasise ensure exclude demonstrate
illustrate invalidate justify link maximise shift

Example:

Word   **Example sentence**

comment: _____ Experts **commented** that the report was full of errors. _____

_____

_____

_____

_____

_____

_____

_____

_____

Verbs followed by "wh~ word + clause"

The following verbs can also be used with a "wh~ word + clause": *illustrate, demonstrate, emphasise, specify.*

Example:

- *The engineer **demonstrated** how the new equipment worked.*

7.8 Make correct sentences using these verbs by putting the words below in the right order. The first word in each sentence is in bold.

Example:

The following example / in practice / how / this / illustrates / operates

The following example illustrates how this operates in practice.

a) important / illustrates / is / how / Middle Eastern / religion / **This** story / in / culture

b) operates / will attempt to / **This** section / how / the Stock Exchange / demonstrate

c) work / **Regulations** / drivers / can / how many hours / specify

d) to use / software / will be / how / **They** / the latest / demonstrating

e) **The** contract / is not covered / clearly specifies / by the agreement / who

f) a small company like this one / of this presentation / increase profits / to illustrate / is / can / **The** purpose / how

Task 8: Review time

It is important you find time to review the exercises you have done in this unit and to review what you have learnt.

8.1 Look back through the unit and find:
  a) five "adjective + noun" collocations;
  b) five "noun + noun" collocations;
  c) five nouns often followed by prepositions;
  d) five words that can be either nouns or verbs.

8.2 Look back over all the exercises you have done and write down phrases that you think are useful and that you want to remember.

Examples:

… clearly illustrates the point …
… an enormous shift in attitudes …
… has decreased noticeably …
… focusing on research and development …
… make a positive contribution …
… expand rapidly …
… an over-generalised conclusion …

Write your own notes and phrases here.

_____

_____

_____

_____

_____

8.3 Look at AWL Sublist 3 at the back of this book. Check if there are any words that you have not met in this unit and that you do not know. Check the words in your dictionary and make notes on the meaning and how to use the word.

Example:

Word (word class)	Meaning
consensus (noun)	• an opinion that everyone in a group agrees with or accepts

Example phrases:

… a lack of consensus
… consensus that …
… failed to reach a consensus on …
… the current consensus of opinion …
The general consensus was that …

Example sentence:

*There is a general **consensus** among teachers that children should have a broad understanding of the world.*

Your notes on other words:

_____

_____

_____

_____

_____

_____

_____

Vocabulary List

Business and Finance
domestic market
economic regeneration
existing market
export strategy
imports
Ministry of Finance
profitability

Environment
Antarctica
conservationist
fossil fuel
harmful substance
industrial pollution
rainfall
reservoir
solar energy
tidal energy
toxicity
waste disposal plant
wind energy

Health
health worker
invasive surgery
medical facility
medical procedure
passive smoking
pharmaceuticals
sufferer

Manufacturing
component
electrical part
electronic circuit
fully guaranteed
goods
liability
manufacturer
repair work
research and development
semiconductor
technical specification

Politics
government minister
government scheme

Research
public opinion
survey (n)

Science
ape
baboon
biological basis
carbon dating
dominant male
Earth's core
earthquake
fossil
metal implement
motor behaviour
observation
pioneer
primate
Richter Scale
seed
shellfish
theory of evolution

Society
colonisation
ethnic minority
immigrant
immigration
peer pressure
population density
voluntary worker

Verbs
abandon
account (for)
adapt
break out
compensate
constrain
contribute (to)

convene
coordinate
correspond
deduce
demonstrate
dominate
encourage
exclude
experience
illustrate
implement
imply
interact
justify
lay (emphasis on)
lead
locate
predict
prohibit
publish
release
retain
reveal
smelt
specify
wander

Other
accommodation
aid agency
ancient
applicant
commitment
complication
consensus
constant
core
criterion
deduction
disaster
enthusiasm
entry criteria
error of judgement
existing
framework

implication
infrastructure
initial
insurgent
layer
likely cause
logical sequence
loyal
malfunctioning
negotiation
nonetheless
outcome
over-generalised
parental consent
personnel
phase
prior consent
probable
profound
proportion
proportional
provocation
publicity
reaction
relief effort
remains (n)
responsibility
riot
risk-taking
safety standards
scheme
seniority
shift (n)
surroundings
troops
valid
victim
weapon

9 AWL – Sublist 4

This unit will help you:
- familiarise yourself with the word families in AWL Sublist 4;
- practise understanding and using these words in context.

Task 1: Meanings of words

1.1 Study the words in bold in the extracts below and then do the matching exercise that follows.

Switzerland is a good example of a country where different forms of transport have been fully **integrated**. A transport strategy has been **implemented** which fully coordinates timetables for different forms of transport. For example, buses are timetabled to meet arriving trains, and **subsequent** waiting times are kept to a minimum. The country has adopted an **overall** strategy for transport, and other forms of transport such as boat services and funicular railways are also included.

Excessive pollution in some urban areas has been **attributed** to emissions from diesel and petrol engines, and it is **apparent** that the use of private cars has increased rapidly over the past 30 years. Air pollution is reaching unprecedented levels in some areas, **hence** the need for urgent measures to limit it. Some local authorities would like to **impose** strict limits on the use of cars. They feel that the measures currently in force are simply not **adequate**. They already have considerable powers to deal with traffic problems. For example, in some towns and cities illegally parked cars may be removed without **prior** notice.

Match the words on the left with the definitions on the right.

Example:

Word	Meaning
subsequent	*following on from or coming after something else*

Word	Meaning
subsequent	for this reason or as a result of this
overall	good enough or sufficient for a specific purpose
impose	to make something happen that has been officially decided
hence	to believe that a situation or event is caused by something
adequate	happening previous to a particular time
prior	following on from or coming after something else
implement	to force people to accept something
attribute	when two or more suitable things are connected to work together, more effectively than before
integrate	obvious or easy to notice
apparent	including everything or considering something as a whole

1.2 Complete the pairs of sentences below with the words from Exercise 1.1. In each pair you need the same word for both sentences. In the case of verbs, a different ending may be needed for the word, e.g., ~s, ~ed, ~ing. In the case of nouns you have to decide whether the singular or plural form is appropriate.

Example:

The ___subsequent___ spread of the disease to other regions of the country suggested that it was more virulent than first thought.

After patients have been vaccinated, the ___subsequent___ side-effects may be unpleasant in some cases.

a) Energy policy should be _____ with transport planning.

Urban transportation can easily be _____ with national rail systems.

b) Distribution costs are a major factor, _____, the location of the distribution centre is an important consideration.

Overseas sales are growing rapidly, _____ the need for a second distribution centre.

c) The government will _____ a ban on the import of meat obtained from exotic animals.

Courts can _____ a fine or even a prison sentence for the importation of prohibited foodstuffs.

d) We were not asked to provide details but simply the _____ picture.

Having listened to our presentation, they seemed happy with the _____ approach we had taken.

e) He _____ his long life to the fact that he had never smoked and hadn't touched alcohol for more than 60 years.

His emotional problems can be _____ to his difficult childhood.

f) The office is quite small but it's perfectly _____ for two people.

Unfortunately, we didn't receive _____ training in the use of the software.

g) EU member states are required to _____ regulations passed by the European Parliament.

They have decided to _____ the committee's recommendations in full.

h) Students with no _____ knowledge of the subject may apply for this course.

Flights are often cancelled without _____ warning due to adverse weather conditions.

i) It was soon _____ that there was a serious problem with the equipment.

The flight was cancelled for no _____ reason.

Task 2: Multi-meaning words

2.1 The words in bold in the sentences below have at least two meanings. Look at how they are used and choose the correct meaning.

Example:

The course lays particular **stress** on the need for individual research projects.

a) a feeling of pressure about your work or social life that can stop you relaxing

b) force or pressure applied to an object that can break it or make it change its shape

c) special emphasis given to something

Answer: *c) special emphasis given to something*

1 The court of arbitration is a **mechanism** for settling disputes between companies and trade unions.

   a) an assembly of mechanical items

   b) a way of addressing a problem or getting something done

   c) a structure or behaviour that enables a person to deal with a difficult situation or problem

2 According to the criminal **code**, offences of this nature do not normally result in imprisonment.

   a) a system of rules and regulations that dictate people's behaviour

   b) a system where words and numbers are substituted with others to enable people to send secret messages

   c) a number that comes before a telephone number to show the reciever's area

3 Doctors have to perform a **series** of tests before major surgery can take place.

   a) a succession of things that happen one after the other, but are not necessarily connected

   b) a television or radio programme that appears in sequential parts

   c) a run of matches that two teams play against each other over a time period

4 The **output** of the Canadian oilfields is predicted to rise dramatically in the next ten years.

   a) the quantity of something that can be produced by a person, machine or organisation

   b) the data displayed on a computer screen or printed on to paper from it

   c) the volume of electricity or power a piece of equipment can produce

5 The object is represented in this diagram in three **dimensions**.

   a) a factor in a situation (synonym = aspect)

   b) the measurement, for example, the length, height or width of something

6 Regular exercise **promotes** good health and normal sleep patterns.

   a) to support something to further its progress

   b) to advance someone to a preferable, more responsible job within an organisation

   c) to encourage people to support or use something

7 Almost half the time some teachers spend at school is **occupied** with paperwork.

   a) if something occupies your mind, you think about that thing all the time

   b) if something occupies your time, you are busy doing it

   c) if someone occupies a building or an area of land, they use it

8 The military **regime** is highly unpopular and there are signs it is losing its grip on power.

   a) a government that is in power in a country, often unelected and ruling in a strict way

   b) a special exercise and dietary plan that is intended to improve your health

   c) a rule structure that controls a particular area of life

9 The future **status** of the Serbian province of Kosovo is still uncertain.

   a) the social or professional rank of a person, when compared to other people

   b) the position of an entity, in legal terms

   c) a situation at a particular time, usually in a discussion or argument

10 Initially, the company **concentrated** solely on book distribution but it has now expanded its operations to include music and films.

   a) to think very carefully about something that you are doing

   b) to exist mainly in large groups unspecified areas

   c) to give most or all of your attention to something

Task 3: Word classes

3.1 Check the following words in a dictionary. Then complete the table with the word class they belong to, i.e., noun, verb, adjective or adverb. Some words belong in more than one class.

Word	Word class
stress	*verb, noun*
grant	
hypothesis	
civil	
contrast	
cycle	

Word	Word class
internal	
resolve	
principal	
access	
label	
phase	

3.2 Decide what word class would fill each gap in the following sentences. Write *v* (verb), *n* (noun) or *adj* (adjective) in the brackets after each gap.

Example

The life _____ (_n_) of many insects is extremely short.

Social Science

a) The idea that there is a link between climate and life expectancy is an interesting _____ (—).

b) In certain urban areas of Scotland, alcohol and smoking are the _____ (—) causes of disease in adult males.

c) Although many people have _____ (—) to expert advice on diet and lifestyle, few people take advantage of this opportunity.

d) Health experts have _____ (—) the need to get the message across more clearly.

e) They see education as the first _____ (—) in the battle to improve public health in this region.

f) It is interesting to _____ (—) diet and lifestyle in different areas of the country.

g) But some experts believe that problems related to alcohol and smoking will be extremely difficult to _____ (—).

h) Children who are _____ (—) "difficult" may get less attention from teachers.

i) Disabled drivers are _____ (—) permission to park closer to shops and services.

j) The problem is an _____ (—) matter and will be dealt with by the social services.

k) Claims for financial compensation can be lodged with the _____ (—) courts.

3.3 Now complete the sentences in Exercise 3.2 with words from Exercise 3.1. In the case of verbs, a different ending may be needed for the word, e.g., ~s, ~ed, ~ing. In the case of nouns you have to decide whether the singular or plural form is appropriate.

Example:

The life _____cycle_____ (n) of many insects is extremely short.

Task 4: Word families

Look at these two sentences.

> We might want to use our knowledge that four feet is the average height in this child's class to **predict** the average height in another class.

> The two chief concerns of statistics are with (1) **summarizing** our experience so that we and other people can understand its essential features, and (2) using the **summary** to make estimates or **predictions** about what is likely to be the case in other (perhaps future) situations.

Source: Slaght, J., Harben, P., Pallant, A. (2006). *English for Academic Study: Reading and Writing Source Book*. Reading: Garnet Education.

The highlighted words *predict* and *prediction* come from the same word family, as do the words *summary* and *summarising*. As we have seen in previous units, this use of members of the same word family helps the writer make the writing more cohesive.

4.1 Put the words in the box below into the table with other members of their families. Remember that you may not be able to complete every column for each word, but there may be some columns where there are two entries.

| subsequently   accessible   annually   concentration   promotion |
| debatable   investigation   occupation   predictable   statistically |
| optional   apparently   occupational   predictably |

Nouns	Verbs	Adjectives	Adverbs
		subsequent	subsequently
	concentrate		
		annual	
	promote		

Nouns	Verbs	Adjectives	Adverbs
debate			
	predict		
statistics			
	investigate		
	occupy		
option			
		apparent	
access			

4.2 Choose the correct form of the word in brackets to complete the following sentences. In the case of verbs, a different ending may be needed for the word, e.g., ~s, ~ed, ~ing. In the case of nouns you have to decide whether the singular or plural form is appropriate.

Example:

Company accounts are audited ____annually____. (annual)

Transport

a) The authorities are carrying out a full _____ into the incident when two airplanes passed within 100 metres of each other above London. (investigate)

b) According to _____, you are far less likely to die in a plane crash than in any other regular means of transport. (statistics)

c) The long-term effects of the rapid increase in low-cost air travel are not _____ at this stage. (predict)

d) The rise of budget airlines in Europe has meant that cheap air travel is now _____ to almost everyone in the European Union. (access)

e) High _____ of pollutants have been found around some airports. (concentrate)

a

Business and Finance

f) The survey found a sharp fall in the number of people in manual _____ . (occupy)

g) It also found that young males were more interested in high pay and _____ than older people, and less worried about job security. (promote)

h) People with no academic qualifications often have no _____ but to take low-paid unattractive work. (option)

i) It is _____ whether an economy based on service industries can provide long-term stability in employment. (debate)

j) The factory closed five years ago but the _____ effects on the local community are still being felt. (subsequent)

k) _____ the potential effects of the closure were not taken into consideration at the time. (apparent)

> **Language note:** The two main varieties of English, American and British English are very similar. With increased globalisation, some of the contrasts are disappearing, e.g., *aeroplane* is being increasing replaced in British English by the American *airplane*.

> **Study tip:** For more information on word families, refer back to Unit 3.

Lexical cohesion

As we said in the introduction to this task, writers often use words from the same family to make their texts cohesive.

4.3 Complete each sentence with a family member of the word in brackets.

Example:

Scientists have been _investigating_ the causes of global warming. Their _investigations_ have reached a number of different conclusions. (investigate)

a) Early in 2006, Parliament _____ the introduction of identity cards. The _____ was often inconclusive and finally a compromise was reached. (debate)

b) The entrance to the museum has been widened to give improved _____ for disabled people. However, many of the other public buildings in the city are still not fully _____ to people in wheelchairs. (access)

c) During the Second World War, the Germans _____ France. Many French people consider the _____ to be the most painful period in French history. (occupy)

d) Some scientists _____ that the Earth's temperature will rise by as much as 5°C over the next 20 years. Other scientists dispute these _____, however. (predict)

e) The _____ into the cause of the crash is continuing. The _____ say it could take several weeks to complete. (investigate)

f) Good _____ skills are essential in the modern world, but many employers have found that school leavers are relatively poor _____. (communicate)

Task 5: Prefixes

The following prefixes are used with a number of the words from the AWL Sublist 4.

Prefix	Meaning
re~	again
in~, un~	not, the opposite of

5.1 Which of the above prefixes can be used with the following words?

Example:

accessible ___inaccessible___

a) adequate _____

b) communicative _____

c) cycle _____

d) resolved _____

e) predictable _____

5.2 Complete the following sentences using either:

● the word in brackets; or

● a prefix + the word in brackets.

In the case of verbs you should choose the correct ending, e.g., *~ed*, *~ing*, *~s*.

Example:

Unfortunately there is ___inadequate___ provision for the recycling of waste in this area. (adequate)

Environment

b

a) Countries like Canada are planning to _____ almost 100 percent of their waste. (cycle)

b) Local authorities must provide _____ waste disposal facilities. (adequate)

c) If we continue to produce waste at the current rate, we are facing an _____ future. (predictable)

d) Problems with the disposal of non-recyclable items such as batteries remain _____. (resolved)

e) One of the main difficulties we face is that the person charged with selling the idea of recycling to the public is an unresponsive and _____ individual. (communicative)

Task 6: Collocations

Verbs and nouns

Look at these "verb + noun" combinations that appear in this unit.

● *impose limits*

● *promotes good health*

6.1 Match the verbs on the left with the nouns on the right to make combinations that can all be found in the previous exercises in this unit. Some verbs should be combined with more than one noun.

Example:

grant permission (Exercise 3.2, sentence i)

Verb	Noun
occupy	a strategy
grant	a ban
implement	the need
impose	the causes
give	France
stress	an investigation
carry out	no option
have	recommendations
investigate	a fine
	limits
	access
	permission

6.2 Choose one verb from the box that fits best with all the nouns in each group.

commit	predict	~~promote~~	retain	stress	undertake

Examples:

promote	development, growth, awareness, health
a) _____	outcome, the future, the weather, rain, growth
b) _____	independence, staff, control, heat
c) _____	a crime, a robbery, an offence, suicide
d) _____	the need, the importance, the urgency, the value
e) _____	an action, an analysis, a project, a task

6.3 Complete the sentences below with an appropriate "verb + noun" combination from Exercise 6.2. The first letter of each noun is given to help you. Pay attention to the form and tense of the verb in each sentence.

Example:

The use of fertiliser _promotes_ plant _growth_ .

a) The government intends to _____ c_____ over the security forces.

b) Nutritionists _____ the i_____ of a balanced diet.

c) Dr Johnson _____ the enormous t_____ of compiling the first comprehensive English dictionary.

d) Men _____ far more violent c_____ than women.

e) Economists are _____ very low g_____ for the first quarter of the next financial year.

Adjectives and nouns

6.4 Match the adjectives on the left with the nouns on the right to make combinations that can all be found in the previous exercises in this unit.

Example:

subsequent spread (Exercise 1.3)

Adjective	Noun
subsequent	notice
prior	provision
internal	concern
inadequate	matter
overall	strategy
chief	spread

6.5 Which nouns are commonly used with these adjectives? Find some matching nouns in your dictionary.

Example:

statistical   _analysis, method, technique_ _____

a) emerging   _____

b) overall   _____

c) internal   _____

d) adequate   _____

e) domestic   _____

f) prior   _____

g) civil   _____

h) hypothetical   _____

i) principal   _____

Discovering collocations

You will learn a lot of collocations by paying attention to the way words are used in texts.

6.6 Look at the words in bold in the following sentences. Identify different combinations of verbs, nouns, adjectives, adverbs and prepositions. Then answer the question that follows.

a) **Statistics** show that the number of people voting in local elections is falling steadily.

b) The findings confirmed the **hypothesis** that smokers are at greater risk of heart attack.

c) Some experts have rejected the **hypothesis** linking smoking with several other fatal diseases.

d) It's too early to make any **predictions** about the make-up of the next government.

e) This task requires a peaceful environment and total **concentration**.

f) Stockbrokers need direct **access** to the latest financial data.

g) We place particular **stress** on first-class customer service.

h) It was discovered that the forensic scientist had committed a serious **error**.

i) It is extremely difficult to break the **cycle** of violence caused by drug abuse.

j) These documents have no legal **status** in Britain.

k) The government is hoping to achieve their **goal** of providing a computer for every classroom.

l) What other **options** do we have?

Question

What verbs are used with these nouns (either before or after)?

Example:

	stress	_place **stress**_
a)	access	_____
b)	hypothesis	_____
c)	statistics	_____
d)	predictions	_____
e)	concentration	_____
f)	error	_____
g)	cycle	_____
h)	status	_____
i)	options	_____
j)	goals	_____

6.7 Look at the words in bold in the following sentences. Identify different combinations of verbs, nouns, adjectives, adverbs and prepositions. Then answer the questions that follow.

a) Statistical data can be used to make realistic economic **predictions**.

b) According to official **statistics**, only 25 percent of the electorate turned out to vote.

c) The latest **prediction** is that 80 percent of households will have a PC within five years.

d) Students embarking on degree courses need to be able to **communicate** effectively in both speech and writing.

e) The drug is still in the experimental **phase** and has not yet been subjected to clinical trials.

f) There was a high **concentration** of alcohol in the victim's bloodstream.

g) This is a fully **integrated** system.

h) The book makes economics easily **accessible** to the general reader.

i) A number of people in the company are under a lot of **stress** right now and have little time to relax.

j) Many people have problems dealing with the emotional **stress** of divorce.

k) The new products are aggressively **promoted** and marketed.

l) This approach **contrasts** sharply with the methods used by the previous marketing manager.

m) The objective is to adjust the results so that the **error** in the statistics is minimised.

n) Lawyers have traditionally enjoyed high social **status**.

o) Students must have definite **goals** towards which they can work.

Questions

a) What adjectives are used before these nouns?

_____ statistics

_____ phase

_____ concentration

_____ stress

_____ predictions

_____ status

_____ goals

b) What prepositions are used before these nouns?

_____ statistics

_____ stress

_____ phase

c) What adverbs are used with these words either before or after?

integrated _____

promote _____

accessible _____

communicate _____

contrast _____

Task 7: Word grammar

Discovering noun patterns

You have studied the following patterns in Unit 5: Word grammar. Exercise 7.1 will help you notice these patterns in the texts you read.

- noun + preposition, e.g., *attitudes towards*
- noun followed by that, e.g., *prediction that*
- noun followed by "*to* + infinitive", e.g., *commitment to reduce*

7.1 Look at the words in bold in the sentences below and identify:

- what prepositions are used to connect the nouns to following nouns;
- which nouns are followed by "*that* + clause" (or *is/are* + *that* + clause);
- which bold noun is followed by a preposition + *wh~* word + clause;
- what preposition comes before *contrast;*
- which nouns are followed by "*to* + infinitive";
- which bold word is not a noun, what word class it is and what comes after this word.

a) The government is bringing in new laws in order to change **attitudes** towards the employment of older people.

_____

_____

_____

b) Many people take the **attitude** that people over 60 years of age are no longer useful to society.

_____

_____

_____

c) There is clearly an **error** in the data.

_____

_____

_____

d) The decision to relocate the company was an **error** of judgement.

_____

_____

_____

e) The latest **prediction** is that 80 percent of households will have a PC within five years.

_____

_____

_____

f) **Predictions** of violence in the run-up to the elections are growing.

g) There was a lot of **debate** about whether the elections should go ahead as planned.

Language note: *Job* in this situation means "a specific responsibility".

h) It's the teacher's **job** to ensure that students are well-prepared for the exam.

i) The government has made a **commitment** to reduce traffic congestion in major cities.

j) They say they have a strong **commitment** to cheap and efficient public transport.

k) The **contrast** between the north and the south of the country is very evident.

l) Unemployment is still rising in the north, in **contrast** to the south, where it is falling steadily.

m) The university has several **mechanisms** for settling disputes.

n) Students usually have no **option** but to live in rented accommodation.

_____

_____

o) She went to work **despite** the fact that she had a high temperature.

_____

_____

p) **Despite** extensive treatment, the patient's condition failed to improve.

_____

_____

q) The average life **cycle** of some insects is incredibly short.

_____

_____

r) The findings support the **hypothesis** that smokers run a greater risk of contracting heart disease.

_____

_____

"Noun + noun" combinations

Here are some more examples of "noun + noun" combinations from previous exercises in this unit.

- _transport strategy_
- _heart disease_
- _diesel engine_
- _air pollution_

7.2   Match nouns from the left and right columns to make "noun + noun" combinations that can be found in the preceding exercises in this unit.

Example:

energy policy (Exercise 1.3, sentence a)

Noun 1	Noun 2
energy	conditions
life	sentence
distribution	union
prison	costs
weather	expectancy
research	policy
trade	project

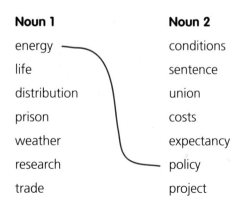

7.3 Check in your dictionary and find nouns that can be used in combination with the following nouns (either before or after).

Example:

code   *area, security, computer, bar, name*

a) error

b) project

c) mechanism

> **Study tip:** For more information about noun patterns, see Unit 4: Collocations.

Adjectives + clauses or verb phrases

We have already seen in this and previous units that both verbs and nouns can be followed by clauses. Some adjectives can also be followed by "(*that*) + clause" or by a phrase.

Examples:

- We are **confident that** the stadium will be finished in time.
- It's **normal to feel** nervous before visiting the dentist.
- It's **worth** talking to your tutor before making a final decision.

Discovering adjective patterns

7.4 Look at the following sentences and notice particularly the way the highlighted adjectives are connected to what follows them. Then answer the questions that follow.

a) Funds may be **available** to assist students who want to study abroad.

b) This car is much more **economical** to drive than other cars in the same class.

c) It was **evident** that drugs were involved.

d) It is **illegal** for anyone in this country to possess or sell narcotics.

e) It is highly **significant** that many of these crimes are committed by drug users.

f) It would not be **appropriate** for me to make that decision.

g) It seems **appropriate** that we should start with a review of the past year.

h) His friends thought it was **abnormal** for anyone to be so obsessed by weapons.

i) She's absolutely **positive** (that) she hasn't made a mistake.

j) It is **traditional** to eat fish on Good Friday.

k) It may be **valid** to use these statistics in isolation.

l) The amount is not **sufficient** to cover all our costs.

m) It is **apparent** that we have a major problem.

n) It is **debatable** whether some alternative medicines actually work.

o) It seems **obvious** that tax rises affect inflation.

p) In the current economic climate it is fairly **predictable** that inflation will continue to rise.

Questions

a) Which adjectives are used with "*that* + clause"?

b) Which adjectives are used with "*for* (*someone*) + *to* + infinitive"?

> **Language note:** The phrase … *for someone* … can be added to most of these adjectives, with the possible exception of *valid*.

c) Which adjectives are used with "*to* + infinitive"?

d) What is different about the pattern used after *debatable*?

> **Language note:** The phrase … *for someone* … is optional. It is possible to drop it and say, e.g., *it is illegal to develop biological weapons*.

Transitive or intransitive verbs

In earlier exercises in this unit we have seen examples of the following verbs which show that they can be used with noun phrases as objects: *attribute, commit, grant, implement, impose, integrate, label, occupy, predict, promote, resolve, retain, stress, undertake*.

Examples:

- *Different forms of transport have been fully **integrated**.*
- *Excessive pollution has been **attributed** to emissions from petrol and diesel engines.*
- *Children who are **labelled** "difficult" may get less attention from teachers.*

Notice that in these examples the three verbs are used passively. All transitive verbs can be used passively.

7.5 Here are some other example sentences from previous exercises. Indicate whether the verbs are used in passive or active form.

Example:

Some local authorities would like to **impose** strict limits on the use of cars. _____active_____

a) A transport strategy has been **implemented** which fully coordinates timetables for different forms of transport. _____

b) Regular exercise **promotes** good health and normal sleep patterns. _____

c) Almost half the time teachers spend at school is **occupied** with paperwork. _____

d) The US plans to **retain** control over the security forces. _____

7.6 Here are some other verbs from AWL Sublist 4 which are always transitive and others which are always intransitive. Complete the table below by putting the verbs in the box in the correct column.

~~access~~ domesticate emerge implicate internalise

Transitive verbs	Intransitive verbs
access	

7.7 Copy an example sentence from your dictionary for each of the transitive verbs from the completed table in Exercise 7.6.

Example:

access: the database can be accessed via any of the workstations.

7.8 Copy an example sentence from your dictionary for each of the intransitive verbs from the completed table in Exercise 7.6.

Example:

emerge: New evidence has emerged that calls the verdict into question.

Language note: Verbs sometimes have different meanings when used transitively or intransitively.

Verbs that are both transitive and intransitive

The following verbs are sometimes transitive and sometimes intransitive: *commit, communicate, concentrate, confer, contrast, resolve, project, summarise.*

7.9 Look at the verbs as they are used in these sentences and decide if they are transitive (VT) or intransitive (VI).

Example:

More people **communicate** with each other by e-mail than by letter. (_VI_)

a) It is still not known exactly how the virus is **communicated**. (__)

b) German speakers are **concentrated** mainly in the northeast of Italy. (__)

c) The report **concentrated** on bilingual education. (__)

d) The study **contrasts** the educational achievements of bilingual and monolingual children. (__)

e) The relatively small amount of waste recycled in Britain **contrasts** sharply with that of Canada and Switzerland. (__)

f) Officials are **projecting** a ten percent increase in the amount of glass recycled over the next five years. (__)

g) The jetty is 500 metres long and **projects** more than 400 metres into the sea. (__)

h) Table 4.7 **summarises** the connection between climate and crop yields. (__)

i) To **summarise**, in most cases yields were higher in years with higher rainfall. (__)

j) After the earthquake the authorities **resolved** to rebuild the city. (__)

k) The question of compensation has finally been **resolved**. (__)

l) A lot of money has been **committed** to the reconstruction of the city. (__)

Verbs followed by "(*that*) + clause"

In earlier exercises you will have seen that some verbs can be followed by "(*that*) + clause", for example, in Exercise 4.3:

● *Some scientists **predict that** the Earth's temperature will rise by as much as 5°C over the next 20 years.*

and in Exercise 3.2:

● *Some experts **believe that** problems related to alcohol and smoking will be extremely difficult to resolve.*

7.10 Check in your dictionary and circle the words in the box that can be used with "(*that*) + clause". Copy example sentences from your dictionary.

> communicate   debate   emerge   hypothesise   (predict)
>
> project   resolve   stress

Example:

Word   **Example sentence**

predict: Industry experts **predict** that another 600 pubs will close by the end of the year.

_____

_____

_____

_____

_____

Verbs followed by "*wh~* word + clause"

Only two verbs from AWL Sublist 4 can be followed by "*wh~* word + clause": *predict, debate*.

Example:

● *Ministers **have been debating whether** to raise taxes.*

7.11 Find other example sentences in your dictionary where these two verbs are used in the same way and copy them below.

_____

_____

_____

_____

Task 8: Review time

It is important you find time to review the exercises you have done in this unit and also review what you have learnt.

8.1 Look back through the unit and find:

a) five "adjective + noun" collocations

b) five "noun + noun" collocations

c) five nouns often followed by prepositions

d) five words that can be either nouns or verbs

8.2 Look back over all the exercises you have done and write down phrases that you think are useful and that you want to remember.

Examples:

… to impose strict limits on …
… the measures currently in force …
… is predicted to rise dramatically …
… few people take advantage of this opportunity …
… were not taken into consideration …
… in the experimental phase …
… easily accessible to …
… despite the fact that …
… support this hypothesis …

Write your own words and phrases here.

_____

_____

_____

_____

_____

_____

_____

_____

8.3 Look at AWL Sublist 4 at the back of this book. Check if there are any words that you have not met in this unit and that you still do not know. Check them in your dictionary and make notes on the meanings and how to use the words.

Example:

Word (word class)	Meaning
ethnic (adjective)	• relating to a particular race, nation or tribe and its customs and traditions

Example phrases:

ethnic groups, ethnic background, ethnic divisions, ethnic cooking, ethnic cleansing

Your notes on other words:

_____

_____

_____

_____

_____

_____

_____

_____

_____

_____

Vocabulary List

Business and Finance
budget airline
customer service
distribution centre
distribution costs
economic climate
economist
financial year
importation
oilfield
service industry
stockbroker
tax rise
trade union

Education
academic qualification
bilingual education
degree course
monolingual
school leaver

Environment
air pollution
disposal
energy policy
fertiliser
non-recyclable items
pollutant
recycling

Health
alternative medicine
balanced diet
bloodstream
clinical trial
condition
drug abuse
fatal disease
heart attack
life expectancy
lifestyle
major surgery
narcotics
nutritionist
regular exercise
sleep pattern
virulent

Law
civil court
claim (*n*)
court of arbitration
criminal code

dispute (*n*)
divorce (*n*)
evidence
financial compensation
imprisonment
lawyer
legal position
legal status
offence
prison sentence
robbery
verdict

Politics
committee
electorate
European Parliament
local authority
local election
military regime
province

Science
experimental phase
forensic scientist
insect
life cycle

Society
ethnic background
ethnic cleansing
ethnic division
ethnic group
identity card
local community
social services
urban area

Verbs
attribute
audit
behave
call (into question)
commit
compile
concentrate
confer
contrast
dispute
divorce
domesticate
embark
emerge
exist

expand
govern
grant
implicate
impose
integrate
internalise
label
link
lodge
minimise
occupy
project
promote
recycle
resolve
settle (a dispute)
summarise
take (into consideration)
turn out
vaccinate
vote

Other
abnormal
access (*n*)
accessible
adequate
analysis
annual
apparent
awareness
ban (*n*)
biological weapon
closure
communication skills
comprehensive
compromise (*n*)
concentration
consideration
contrast (*n*)
crop yield
database
debatable
despite
dimension
disabled driver
emotional problem
excessive
exotic animal
expert advice
extensive
facilities
foodstuffs
fully integrated

Good Friday
grant (*n*)
grip (*n*)
hence
hypothesis
hypothetical
in full
incident
inconclusive
internal
isolation (in ~)
job security
long-term effects
make-up
manual occupation
mechanism
obsessed
occupational
optional
output
overall
paperwork
period (of history)
permission
predictable
prediction
principal
prior notice
prior warning
professional
prohibited
promotion
provision
recommendation
reconstruction
run-up
security forces
series
social status
stability
statistically
stress (*n*)
subsequent
suicide
traditional
traffic congestion
unelected
unpleasant
unprecedented
unresponsive
urban
urgency
violent
workstation

10 AWL – Sublist 5

This unit will help you:
- familiarise yourself with the word families in AWL Sublist 5;
- practise understanding and using these words in context.

Task 1: Meanings of words

1.1 Study the words in bold in the sentences below and then do the matching exercise that follows.

Environment

a) People are becoming increasingly **aware** of the potential damage to the environment caused by the rapid increase in budget air travel.

b) Reducing carbon emissions is a **challenge** faced by all governments in the modern era.

c) Many activists are calling on governments to **enforce** laws governing environmental damage more stringently.

d) Switching to non-fossil fuel **substitutes** could cost billions but the long-term benefits are considerable.

e) Reducing the amount of fossil fuels being burnt is one of the **fundamental** tasks governments will face in the coming decade.

Travel

f) If present **trends** continue, the number of airline passengers is expected to increase by 60 percent in the next ten years.

g) Cheap air travel for all has become a **symbol** of the first years of the 21st century.

h) Experts are becoming increasingly concerned about the **welfare** of passengers who travel frequently on long-haul flights.

i) Analysts believe a tax on aviation fuel would push up the cost of air travel and would also bring in a large amount of tax **revenue** for the government.

j) Others argue that people will have to **modify** their travel habits, taking more holidays at home and using other "greener" forms of transport.

Business and Finance

k) The company structure does not **facilitate** efficient work flow.

l) Exchange-rate **stability** depends on a number of factors, including inflation and bank lending rates.

m) Making the **transition** to a market economy has proved difficult for some of the former Soviet states.

n) The **ratio** of employees to managerial staff is only is 5:1 in some organisations.

Match the words on the left with the definitions on the right.

Example:

Word	Meaning
welfare	the health and happiness of people

Word	Meaning
welfare	something which tests a person's energy and determination
fundamental	something that is used instead of the one that you normally use, because the usual one is not available
facilitate	a subtle change or development that seems likely to continue
aware	a person or thing that is thought of as representing a bigger idea
symbol	the health and happiness of people
modify	the monetary gain that a business organisation receives, often from sales
challenge	the state of staying balanced and not altering
trend	to know of something's exsitence
substitute	to ensure someone abides by something
enforce	to allow something to happen in an easier way
stability	to make small changes to something to increase its effectiveness
ratio	the most essential and simple part of something
transition	how two things relate to each other as numbers
revenue	the change from one form or state to another

1.2 Complete the pairs of sentences below with the words from Exercise 1.1. In each pair you need the same word for both sentences. In the case of verbs, a different ending may be needed for the word, e.g., ~s, ~ed, ~ing. In the case of nouns you have to decide whether the singular or plural form is appropriate.

Example:

Warm clothing is _fundamental_ to survival in the mountains.

A _fundamental_ change in attitude is needed if areas of outstanding natural beauty are to be preserved.

a) The strike is believed to have cost the newspaper over £10 million in lost _____.

To make matters worse, it has also lost a lot of advertising _____ as a result of the dispute.

Strike costs £10 million

b) Few people are _____ of the dangers a sudden change in air pressure can cause.

He suddenly became _____ of someone following him.

c) Driving a car all day is no _____ for healthy exercise.

If you can't get any beef, you can use chicken as a _____.

d) The _____ of the whole region is threatened by the rise of nationalism.

The first task of the new government will be to bring some _____ to the economy.

e) The government says it is not responsible for the _____ of its citizens while they are abroad.

This company takes great care to safeguard the _____ of its workforce at all times.

f) After 15 years in the same job I need a new _____.

The problem of global warming is a huge _____ for the leaders of the developed world.

g) Researchers have noticed a _____ that indicates people are spending an increasing amount of money on leisure travel.

A growing _____ in British society is for young people to borrow money to buy property.

h) Nobody _____ the rules in the manager's absence.

Parking regulations will be strictly _____.

i) The seating plan in this aircraft can be _____ to increase or reduce the number of seats available.

The engine has been _____ slightly and now gives a much better performance.

j) The new terminal will greatly _____ travel to and from the capital.

A relaxed and open-minded approach can _____ language learning.

k) The cross is generally regarded as one of the principal _____ of the Christian religion.

In the new democracies of Eastern Europe, _____ of the former communist regimes were quickly removed.

l) The _____ from a communist system to a free market economy proved to be difficult in many of the former Soviet states.

She found it particularly difficult to make the _____ from school to university.

m) The _____ of teachers to pupils in some British primary schools can be as high as 1:35.

The _____ of men to women in the nursing profession is around 1:25.

Task 2: Multi-meaning words

2.1 The words in the box below have at least two meanings. Look at how they are used in the sentences that follow and choose the correct meaning.

~~capacity~~	compound (*n*)	conflict (*n*)	generation	image	margin
monitor (*n*)	network (*n*)	perspective	prime (*adj*)	target (*n*)	version

Example:

Young children often have an extraordinary **capacity** to learn languages.
a) the amount of something that can be put in a receptacle
b) one's ability to do something
c) the maximum amount of goods that an organisation can produce

Answer: b) one's ability to do something

1 Many companies today are operating on extremely tight **margins**.

   a) the column of space down the side of a page

   b) the difference in the number of points between the winners and the losers of a sports event or competition

   c) the difference between what it costs to buy or produce something and its selling price

2 The **prime** cause of heart disease in this country is smoking.

   a) most important; main

   b) of premium quality

   c) stands out as being the most appropriate for a specific purpose

3 Johannesburg is working hard to clean up its **image**.

   a) the general belief that people tend to have of someone or something

   b) what comes into your mind when you think about someone or something

   c) the reflection you see when you look in a mirror

4 The temperature **monitor** ensures that the temperature within the boiler never exceeds the safety limit.

   a) a computer screen

   b) a piece of equipment that measures and records data

   c) a person whose job is to watch an activity or a situation to see how it changes or develops

5 The first **generation** of mobile phones suffered from being extremely bulky and heavy compared with the ones in use today.

   a) the people in society who are of the same or a similar age

   b) a set of items that were developed at a similar time, and are of better quality or usefulness than a previous set

   c) the system of production involved in making something

6 Depending on your personal **perspective**, the group are either terrorists or freedom fighters.

   a) a particular person's approach to thinking about something

   b) to consider something from many angles to decide on it's relevance or accuracy

   c) the art of representation of distance as the eye sees it

7 The **conflict** in the south of the country shows little sign of dying down.

   a) where two or more people or groups don't agree or argue about something

   b) heavy fighting or even war between countries or groups

   c) a situation in which two or more different needs or influences coexist with difficulty

8 The software comes in different **versions** for different types of computer.

   a) a variation of an original

   b) a person's description of an event or thing which may be different from the description given by another person

   c) a way of explaining something that is typical of a particular group, e.g., "the Marxist version of history"

9 Water is a **compound** of oxygen and hydrogen.

   a) a substance found predominantly in chemistry which contains atoms from two or more elements

   b) an enclosed area that contains a group of buildings

   c) a combination of two or more nouns or adjectives, used as a single word

10 Access to the **network** and Internet access is restricted to students holding a membership card.

   a) a system of lines, wires, roads, etc., that join up with each other and are interconnected

   b) a set of computers that are connected to each other so that information can pass between them

   c) people or organisations, etc., that are connected to each other or that work together as a group

11 The sales **targets** for next year have been reduced following this year's poor performance.

   a) something that you are trying to achieve

   b) something you try to hit in a sport or a game

   c) something you plan to attack

Language note: Some words have very different meanings depending on their word class, e.g., *objective*, *prime* and *compound*.

Task 3: Word classes

3.1 Check the following words in a dictionary. Then complete the table with the word class they belong to, i.e., noun, verb, adjective or adverb. Some words belong in more than one class.

Word	Word class
prime	*noun, verb, adjective*
conflict	
decline	
challenge	
contact	
compound	

Word	Word class
monitor	
network	
reject	
objective	
target	
alternate	

3.2 Decide what word class would fill each gap in the following sentences. Write *v* (verb), *n* (noun) or *adj* (adjective) in the brackets after each gap.

Example:

Our application to build a new factory on this site has been _____ (_v_).

a) She visits her family on _____ (__) weekends.

b) Diplomatic efforts to end the _____ (__) are continuing.

c) The programme is designed to _____ (__) a young audience.

d) Many people argue that standards in medical care are, in fact, _____ (__) despite the many advances in medical treatment.

e) If the solution comes into _____ (__) with the eyes, rinse immediately with cold water.

f) It's very difficult to be _____ (__) when your own financial interests are involved.

g) The city is served by a _____ ( ) of tram and suburban railway lines.

h) The _____ (__) of postgraduate research is too much for many students and they often fail to finish their courses.

i) Interest based on the amount of money originally invested and the interest already earned is known as _____ (__) interest.

j) The machine _____ (__) the patient's condition 24 hours a day.

k) Our _____ (__) concern is to ensure that all patients receive the best available treatment.

3.3 Now complete the sentences in Exercise 3.2 with words from Exercise 3.1. In the case of verbs, a different ending may be needed for the word, e.g., ~s, ~ed, ~ing. In the case of nouns, you have to decide whether the singular or plural form is appropriate.

Example:

Our application to build a new factory on this site has been _____rejected_____ (*v*).

Task 4: Word families

Look at the following extract.

> Whether the world is more prone to conflict than it used to be is hard to say. Perhaps we are just more **aware** of violent confrontation in different parts of the world. A famine in remote Sudan gets media coverage whereas a century ago starving populations might die unseen. Today's wars can be watched live on television, like Hollywood action movies. Greater **awareness** of the human consequences of battle may reduce the lust for war – or make it another spectator sport.

Source: Slaght, J., Harben, P., Pallant, A. (2006). *English for Academic Study: Reading and Writing Source Book*. Reading: Garnet Education.

The highlighted words, *aware* and *awareness*, are members of the same word family. As we have seen in previous units, this use of members of the same word family helps the writer make the writing more cohesive.

4.1   Put the words in the box below into the table with other members of their families. Remember that you may not be able to complete every column for each word, but there may be some columns where there are two entries.

modify   symbolic   expansion   logic   adjust   substitution
evolution   sustain   rejection   consultation   precisely

Nouns	Verbs	Adjectives	Adverbs
modification	modify		
symbol			
		sustainable	
	substitute		
		stable	
	reject		
precision			

Nouns	Verbs	Adjectives	Adverbs
	evolve		
			logically
	consult		
	expand		
adjustment			

4.2 Choose the correct form of the word in brackets to complete the following sentences. In the case of verbs, a different ending may be needed for the word, e.g., ~s, ~ed, ~ing. In the case of nouns, you have to decide whether the singular or plural form is appropriate.

Example:

Governments engaged in crop ___substitution___ programmes were promised extra assistance. (substitute)

a) It is _____ impossible to include all the students at the university in the survey. (logic)

b) The long-term _____ of the currency remains the government's prime objective. (stable)

c) There are no current plans to _____ monetary strategy. (alter)

d) Many regions of the country are experiencing rapid economic _____. (expand)

e) Any attempt to reduce taxes would be seen as a _____ gesture from a government which is rapidly losing support. (symbol)

f) Once the _____ for inflation is taken into account, the fall in interest rates is quite small. (adjust)

g) The importance of the city as a regional financial centre has _____ slowly. (evolve)

h) Work of this type requires a high level of _____. (precise)

i) The government's plans are a _____ of the policies of the previous regime. (reject)

j) Their proposals will require some _____ before they can become law. (modify)

k) It is generally believed that Earth cannot _____ more than six billion people. (sustain)

Lexical cohesion

As we said in the introduction to this task, writers often use words from the same family to make their texts cohesive.

4.3   Complete each sentence with a family member of the word in brackets.

Example:

The company is planning to ___expand___ into Eastern Europe but some members of the management team have argued that such an ___expansion___ may not be in the best interests of the company. (expand)

Business and Finance

a) It is often difficult to _____ to a change of career. Some people fail to make the _____ and simply go back to their old job. (adjust)

b) _____ in the exchange rate is a requirement for continued growth. A _____ currency will encourage investment. (stable)

c) In the modern world, businesses need to _____ rapidly and without such an _____ they are unlikely to maintain their market share. (evolve)

Politics

d) Many people are still not _____ of the dangers of landmines despite numerous government initiatives to raise _____ . (aware)

e) The plan has been drawn up in _____ with our Far Eastern partners. We attempted to _____ them at all stages of the project. (consult)

f) Living standards in the area are _____ rapidly. The main reason for this _____ is the continuing armed conflict in the region. (decline)

g) The US government claims that the weapons their planes use are very _____ . The number of civilian casualties on the ground would suggest that this _____ is more theoretical than real. (precise)

Task 5: Prefixes

The following prefixes are used with a number of the words from the AWL Sublist 5.

Prefix	Meaning
re~	again
in~, un~, il~, im~	not, the opposite of

5.1   Which of the above prefixes can be used with the following words?

Example:

adjustment ___readjustment___   d) sustainable _____

a) aware _____   e) monitored _____

b) draft _____   f) precise _____

c) logical _____   g) stability _____

5.2 Complete the following sentences using either:

  ● the word in brackets; or

  ● a prefix + the word in brackets.

In the case of verbs you should choose the correct ending for the word, e.g., ~ed, ~ing, ~s.

Example:

Fear of flying is totally ____illogical____ given that statistics prove it is the safest form of transport. (logical)

Transport

a) We need transport policies that are both environmentally _____ and economically viable. (aware)

b) Parliament rejected the new transport bill so the minister was forced to _____ it. (draft)

c) New technology means that the movements of aircraft can be _____ even more closely than ever before. (monitor)

d) It may be environmentally friendly, but in the modern age moving goods via the canal network is a totally _____ form of transport. (sustainable)

e) Financial _____ in the region is essential for investment in a modern transport system. (stability)

f) Her directions were both complicated and _____, with the result that I was late for the meeting. (precise)

Task 6: Collocations

Verbs and nouns

Look at these "verb + noun" combinations from sentences in the previous exercises in this unit.

  ● *make the transition*   ● *reduce the number*

6.1 Match the verbs on the left with the nouns on the right to make combinations that can all be found in the previous exercises in this unit.

Example:

enforce the law (Exercise 1.1 sentence 3)

Verb	Noun
enforce	welfare
reduce	access
restrict	the transition
make	stability
face	a challenge
threaten	the law
safeguard	awareness
facilitate	a limit
exceed	targets
raise	learning

6.2 Choose one verb from the box that fits best with all the nouns in each group.

| alter | challenge | ~~draft~~ | generate | monitor | pursue | reject | sustain |

Examples:

_____draft_____	legislation, agreement, constitution, letter
a) _____	assumption, authority, decision, leadership
b) _____	economic growth, life, interest, level
c) _____	activity, progress, situation
d) _____	revenue, jobs, new ideas, electricity
e) _____	offer, argument, suggestion, proposal, request
f) _____	career, policy, matter, issue, interests
g) _____	fact, situation, behaviour, way

6.3 Complete the sentences below with an appropriate "verb + noun" combination from Exercise 6.2. The first letter of each noun is given to help you. Pay attention to the form and tense of the verb in each sentence.

Example:

They have set up a commission to _____draft_____ a new _constitution_.

a) The government has _____ a p_____ to prohibit smoking in all workplaces, including bars and restaurants.

b) Service industries have _____ thousands of new j_____ in recent years.

c) After the operation the medical team has to _____ the patient's p_____ extremely carefully.

d) Local residents are unhappy that the court has decided to allow the new road to be built and have said that they plan to _____ the d_____ in a higher court.

e) As well as doing their school work, students are encouraged to _____ their own i_____.

f) The new wind farm will _____ enough e_____ to supply a small town.

Adjectives and nouns

6.4 Match the adjectives on the left with the nouns on the right to make combinations that can all be found in the previous exercises in this unit.

Example:

fundamental tasks (Exercise 1.1, sentence 6)

Adjective	Noun
fundamental	trend
present	awareness
lost	cause
different	revenue
growing	trends
prime	expansion
compound	tasks
greater	interest
rapid economic	versions

6.5 Which nouns are commonly used with these adjectives? Find some matching nouns in your dictionary.

Example:

academic   achievement, subject, standards, qualifications

a) stable

b) external

c) fundamental

d) prime

e) logical

f) objective

g) precise

Discovering collocations

You will learn a lot of collocations by paying attention to the way words are used in texts.

6.6 Look at the words in bold in the following sentences. Identify different combinations of verbs, nouns, adjectives, adverbs and prepositions. Then answer the questions that follow.

Politics

a) The conflict is rapidly **evolving** into a civil war.

b) The United Nations is **monitoring** the situation very closely.

c) Local journalists argue that the conflict has to be seen from a historical **perspective**.

d) The country has found it extremely difficult to make the **transition** from a dependent colony to a democracy.

e) Meanwhile the government is trying to improve its **image** overseas.

f) According to the official **version** of events, the recent clashes in the west of the country were caused by "criminal gangs".

Business and Finance

g) The local economy **expanded** rapidly during the 1980s and 1990s but is currently in a period of crisis.

h) Businessmen and entrepreneurs have frequently come into **conflict** with politicians as new laws are introduced.

i) Many factories in the country are now working at a reduced **capacity**.

j) The company has the **capacity** to build 3,000 cars a month.

k) The same process has been used for almost 20 years with only minor **modifications**.

l) They have made a number of **modifications** to their latest model to maximise passenger safety.

m) They have also made a slight **adjustment** to the engine.

n) Strong sales in the domestic sector have led to plans to **expand** overseas.

o) The company hopes to reach its **target** of 15 percent growth this year.

p) Car buyers are becoming increasingly environmentally **aware**, however.

q) Green issues have given many consumers a new **perspective** on their everyday transport needs.

Questions

a) What verbs are used with these nouns (either before or after)?

an adjustment	*make an adjustment*
transition	
capacity	
image	
conflict (with)	
modifications	
its target	

b) What adjectives are used with these nouns?

adjustment	
(at) ~ capacity	
perspective	
version	
modifications	

c) What adverbs are used with these words (either before or after)?

evolved _____

aware _____

expand _____

monitor _____

> **Language note:** With the verbs *evolved* and *monitor* the adverb could also appear in the other position, i.e., *evolve gradually, closely monitor*.

Task 7: Word grammar

Discovering noun patterns

You have studied the following patterns in Unit 5: Word grammar. Exercise 7.1 will help you notice these patterns in the texts you read.

- noun + preposition, e.g., *decline in*
- noun followed by *that*, e.g., *the notion that*
- noun followed by "*to + infinitive*", e.g., *capacity to invest*
- noun followed by "*to be + that + clause*", e.g. *trend is that*

7.1 Look at the nouns in bold in the sentences below and identify:

- what prepositions are used to connect the bold nouns to following nouns or gerunds (e.g., *hiring*);
- which noun is followed by "*that + clause*";
- which noun is followed by the verb *to be + that + clause*;
- what prepositions come before *consultation* and *target*;
- which noun is followed by "*to + infinitive*".

a) The new Wembley Stadium has a **capacity** of 90,000 seats.

_____

_____

b) The government is concerned about its **capacity** to invest in the country's infrastructure.

_____

_____

c) The **transition** from a state-owned business to a private company can be extremely difficult.

_____

_____

_____

d) There has been a dramatic **decline** in the number of jobs in the manufacturing sector.

_____

_____

e) A lot of money has been invested in promoting a more positive **image** of the country.

_____

_____

f) The **notion** that the country can recover from its economic problems within the next two years is quite absurd.

_____

_____

g) The system in many countries is far removed from classical **notions** of democracy.

_____

_____

h) In recent years there has been a **trend** towards making low-budget films.

_____

_____

i) One worrying **trend** is that criminals are targeting their victims on the Internet.

_____

_____

j) The plans were drawn up in **consultation** with our overseas partners.

_____

_____

k) The company is now ready to meet the **challenges** of a highly competitive market.

_____

_____

l) There has been a significant **expansion** in the number of software companies operating in this field.

_____

_____

m) The rapid **expansion** of Mexico City led to social and economic problems.

_____

_____

n) Many companies operate on a gross profit **margin** of less than five percent.

_____

_____

_____

o) Prolonged **exposure** to other people's cigarette smoke can cause serious health problems.

_____

_____

_____

p) Most people have an **awareness** of the dangers of passive smoking.

_____

_____

_____

q) Millions of dollars have been invested in schemes to raise **awareness** about AIDS in Africa.

_____

_____

_____

r) Sales last year were five percent below **target**.

_____

_____

_____

s) The company says it is on **target** for a 20 percent increase in sales this year.

_____

_____

_____

t) The government will fail to meet its **target** of reducing greenhouse gas emissions by ten percent this year.

_____

_____

_____

7.2 Look back at the previous exercises in this unit and check which prepositions are used to connect these nouns with following nouns or gerunds.

Example:

ratio	*of something to something else*	(Exercise 1.1)
a) welfare		(Exercise 1.1)
b) symbol		(Exercise 1.1)
c) generation		(Exercise 2.1)
d) version		(Exercise 6.6)
e) adjustment		(Exercise 6.6)
f) perspective		(Exercise 6.6)

"Noun + noun" combinations

Here are some examples of "noun + noun" combinations from previous exercises in this unit.

- *budget air travel*
- *market economy*
- *fossil fuels*
- *airline passengers*

7.3 Match nouns from the left and right columns to make "noun + noun" combinations that can be found in the preceding exercises in this unit.

Noun 1	Noun 2
air	fuel
blood	disease
aviation	target
exchange	flow
heart	limit
safety	travel
freedom	rate
Internet	access
sales	rates
interest	fighter

7.4 Check in your dictionary and find nouns that can be used in combination with the following nouns (either before or after).

Example:

target	*sales, production, date, level, audience*	
a) substitute		
b) energy		
c) network		
d) margin		

Discovering adjective patterns

We saw in Unit 9, Exercise 7.4, how some adjectives can be followed by "(*that*) + clause" or by a verb phrase. In this exercise we will look at other adjectives and how they are used in sentences.

7.5 Look at the bold words in the sentences below and identify:

- which adjectives are followed by "*to* + infinitive";
- which adjectives are followed by "*that* + clause";
- which prepositions are used to connect the adjectives to following noun phrases.

Health and keeping fit

a) Twenty minutes' exercise on this machine is **equivalent** to walking five kilometres.

b) Most people are well **aware** that regular exercise promotes good health.

c) They are **aware** of the benefits of a healthy diet combined with exercise.

d) Running or jogging for at least 20 minutes three times a week is **fundamental** to building up a good physical condition.

e) It is **logical** to start with gentle exercise and then build up the routine over a number of weeks.

f) It is difficult to be **precise** about the number of calories different sporting activities can burn off.

g) It may seem **logical** that if output exceeds input you will lose weight but, unfortunately, this does not always happen.

_____

_____

_____

h) The current obsession with dieting is **symbolic** of an age when image is everything.

_____

_____

_____

Transitive or intransitive verbs

In earlier exercises in this unit we have seen examples of the following verbs which show that they can be used with noun phrases as objects: _enforce, facilitate, modify, reject, target, monitor, alter, sustain, draft, challenge, generate, pursue._

Examples:

- _enforce laws_
- _facilitate blood flow_
- _parking regulations will be strictly enforced_
- _modify their travel habits_

Notice that in one of these examples the verb is used passively. All transitive verbs can be used passively.

7.6 Here are some other verbs from AWL Sublist 5 which are either always transitive or always intransitive. Complete the table below by putting the verbs in the correct column.

> ~~amend~~   compound   conflict   contact   enable   expose
> liberalise   license   symbolise

Transitive verbs	Intransitive verbs
amend	

7.7 Copy an example sentence from your dictionary for each of the transitive verbs from the completed table in Exercise 7.6.

Example:

amend: The law was **amended** so that profits from drug dealing could be seized by the government.

_____

_____

_____

_____

_____

_____

_____

_____

_____

_____

_____

_____

_____

_____

_____

_____

_____

7.8 Copy an example sentence from your dictionary for each of the intransitive verbs from the completed table in Exercise 7.6.

_____

_____

_____

_____

_____

_____

_____

_____

_____

_____

_____

_____

_____

_____

_____

_____

Language note: The meaning of a verb can change if it is used transitively or intransitively, e.g., _decline_.

Verbs that are both transitive and intransitive

The following verbs are sometimes transitive and sometimes intransitive: *adjust, alter, consult, decline, expand, evolve, stabilise, substitute*.

7.9 Look at the verbs as they are used in these sentences and decide if they are transitive (VT) or intransitive (VI).

Example:

An increasing number of people are choosing to **alter** their appearance with cosmetic surgery. (*VT*)

a) The latest figures have been **adjusted** to take account of inflation. (__)

b) Businesses need time to **adjust** to changing economic circumstances. (__)

c) The number of people owning their own homes has **declined** by ten percent. (__) ·

d) She **declined** the offer. (__)

e) Businesses must **evolve** new ways of working to keep pace with technological advances. (__)

f) Software will continue to **evolve** as consumers demand more effective solutions. (__)

g) New regulations are needed to help to **stabilise** the economy. (__)

h) Interest rates have now **stabilised**. (__)

i) The manufacturers have stopped using steel and **substituted** a lighter and more flexible material. (__)

j) When gold was discovered in the area, Johannesburg **expanded** rapidly and soon became a thriving city. (__)

k) The university is planning to **expand** the number of overseas students to around 20 percent of the whole student body. (__)

l) More than 500 business managers were **consulted** in the survey. (__)

m) They **consulted** with a number of representatives from different sectors of the economy. (__)

Task 8: Review time

It is important you find time to review the exercises you have done in this unit and also review what you have learnt.

8.1 Look back through the unit and find:

a) five "adjective + noun" collocations

b) five "noun + noun" collocations

c) five nouns often followed by prepositions

d) five words that can be either nouns or verbs

8.2 Look back over all the exercises you have done and write down phrases that you think are useful and that you want to remember.

Examples:

… reject suggestions that …
… nothing can alter the fact that…
… sustain economic growth …
… make a slight adjustment to …
… make the transition from … to …
… expand rapidly …
…. become stable …

Write your own words and phrases here.

_____

_____

_____

_____

_____

_____

_____

_____

8.3 Look at AWL Sublist 5 at the back of this book. Check if there are any words that you have not met in this unit and that you do not know. Check them in your dictionary and make notes on the meaning and how to use the word.

Example:

Word (word class)	Meaning
entity (noun)	something that exists as a separate and complete unit

Example sentences:

*The province has now become a separate **entity**.*

*The four sections have been brought together as a single **entity**.*

Your notes on other words:

_____

_____

_____

_____

_____

_____

_____

_____

Vocabulary List

Business and Finance
advertising
bank lending rate
currency
domestic sector
entrepreneur
financial centre
gross profit margin
interest rate
manufacturing sector
market economy
monetary strategy
revenue
state-owned business
strike (*n*)
tax revenue
work flow

Education
postgraduate research

Environment
carbon emission
environmentally aware
environmentally friendly
green issue
wind farm

Health
heart disease
welfare

Politics
bill
colony
commission

communist regime
constitution
democracy
diplomatic efforts
freedom fighter
government initiative
Marxist
nationalism
terrorist
United Nations

Science
air pressure
atom
chemical substance
element
evolution
hydrogen
oxygen

Society
citizen
living standards
local resident

Verbs
adjust
argue
claim
coexist
consult
die down
earn
enforce
engage (in)
evolve

fail
keep pace (with)
liberalise
license
modify
preserve
pursue
push up
reject
safeguard
substitute
supply
sustain
switch
threaten

Other
absurd
activist
alternate
armed conflict
aviation fuel
aware
bulky
challenge (*n*)
civil war
civilian casualties
claim (*n*)
competitive
compound
considerable
consultation
dependent
description
entity
expansion
exposure

generation
illogical
image
input (*n*)
interconnected
Internet access
journalist
landmine
logic
long-haul flight
margin
modern era
modification
monitor (*n*)
network
notion
open-minded
outstanding natural beauty
perspective
precise
prime objective
prone to
ratio
rejection
safety limit
stringently
substitute (*n*)
substitution
survival
sustainable
symbol
symbolic
target
thriving
transition
version
viable

Appendix 1:
Academic Word List

On the following pages you will find all the members of the word families in the first five sublists of the Academic Word List.

Each word in italics is the most frequently occurring member of the word family in the Academic Corpus. For example, *analysis* is the most common form of the word family 'analyse'. British and American spellings are included in the word families, so 'contextualise' and 'contextualize' are both included in the family *context*.

analyse
analysed
analyser
analysers
analyses
analysing
analysis
analyst
analysts
analytic
analytical
analytically
analyze
analyzed
analyzes
analyzing

approach
approachable
approached
approaches
approaching
unapproachable

area
areas

assess
assessable
assessed
assesses
assessing
assessment
assessments
reassess
reassessed
reassessing
reassessment
unassessed

assume
assumed
assumes
assuming
assumption
assumptions

authority
authoritative
authorities

available
availability
unavailable

benefit
beneficial
beneficiary
beneficiaries
benefited
benefiting
benefits

concept
conception
concepts
conceptual
conceptualisation
conceptualise
conceptualised
conceptualises
conceptualising
conceptually

consist
consisted
consistency
consistent
consistently
consisting
consists
inconsistencies
inconsistency
inconsistent

constitute
constituencies
constituency
constituent
constituents
constituted
constitutes
constituting
constitution
constitutions
constitutional
constitutionally
constitutive
unconstitutional

context
contexts
contextual
contextualise
contextualised
contextualising
uncontextualised
contextualize
contextualized
contextualizing
uncontextualized

contract
contracted
contracting
contractor
contractors
contracts

create
created
creates
creating
creation
creations
creative
creatively
creativity
creator
creators
recreate
recreated
recreates
recreating

data

define
definable
defined
defines
defining
definition
definitions
redefine
redefined
redefines
redefining
undefined

derive
derivation
derivations
derivative
derivatives
derived
derives
deriving

distribute
distributed
distributing
distribution
distributional
distributions
distributive
distributor
distributors

redistribute
redistributed
redistributes
redistributing
redistribution

economy
economic
economical
economically
economics
economies
economist
economists
uneconomical

environment
environmental
environmentalist
environmentalists
environmentally
environments

establish
disestablish
disestablished
disestablishes
disestablishing
disestablishment
established
establishes
establishing
establishment
establishments

estimate
estimated
estimates
estimating
estimation
estimations
over-estimate
overestimate
overestimated
overestimates
overestimating
underestimate
underestimated
underestimates
underestimating

evident
evidenced
evidence
evidential
evidently

export
exported
exporter
exporters
exporting
exports

factor
factored
factoring
factors

finance
financed
finances
financial
financially
financier
financiers
financing

formula
formulae
formulas
formulate
formulated
formulating
formulation
formulations
reformulate
reformulated
reformulating
reformulation
reformulations

function
functional
functionally
functioned
functioning
functions

Identify
identifiable
identification
identified
identifies
identifying
identities
identity
unidentifiable

income
incomes

indicate
indicated
indicates
indicating

indication
indications
indicative
indicator
indicators

individual
individualised
individuality
individualism
individualist
individualists
individualistic
individually
individuals

interpret
interpretation
interpretations
interpretative
interpreted
interpreting
interpretive
interprets
misinterpret
misinterpretation
misinterpretations
misinterpreted
misinterpreting
misinterprets
reinterpret
reinterpreted
reinterprets
reinterpreting
reinterpretation
reinterpretations

involve
involved
involvement
involves
involving
uninvolved

issue
issued
issues
issuing

labour
labor
labored
labors
laboured
labouring
labours

legal
illegal

illegality
illegally
legality
legally

legislate
legislated
legislates
legislating
legislation
legislative
legislator
legislators
legislature

major
majorities
majority

method
methodical
methodological
methodologies
methodology
methods

occur
occurred
occurrence
occurrences
occurring
occurs
reoccur
reoccurred
reoccurring
reoccurs

percent
percentage
percentages

period
periodic
periodical
periodically
periodicals
periods

policy
policies

principle
principled
principles
unprincipled

proceed
procedural

procedure
procedures
proceeded
proceeding
proceedings
proceeds

process
processed
processes
processing

require
required
requirement
requirements
requires
requiring

research
researched
researcher
researchers
researches
researching

respond
responded
respondent
respondents
responding
responds
response
responses
responsive
responsiveness
unresponsive

role
roles

section
sectioned
sectioning
sections

sector
sectors

significant
insignificant
insignificantly
significance
significantly
signified
signifies
signify
signifying

similar
dissimilar
similarities
similarity
similarly

source
sourced
sources
sourcing

specific
specifically
specification

specifications
specificity
specifics

structure
restructure
restructured
restructures
restructuring
structural
structurally
structured
structures
structuring
unstructured

theory
theoretical
theoretically
theories
theorist
theorists

vary
invariable
invariably
variability
variable
variables
variably
variance

variant
variants
variation
variations
varied
varies
varying

Sublist 2

achieve
achievable
achieved
achievement
achievements
achieves
achieving

acquire
acquired
acquires
acquiring
acquisition
acquisitions

administrate
administrates
administration
administrations
administrative
administratively
administrator
administrators

affect
affected
affecting
affective
affectively
affects
unaffected

appropriate
appropriacy
appropriately
appropriateness
inappropriacy
inappropriate
inappropriately

spect
aspects

assist
assistance
assistant
assistants
assisted
assisting
assists
unassisted

category
categories
categorisation
categorise

categorised
categorises
categorising
categorization
categorize
categorized
categorizes
categorizing

chapter
chapters

commission
commissioned
commissioner
commissioners
commissioning
commissions

community
communities

complex
complexities
complexity

compute
computation
computational
computations
computable
computer
computed
computerised
computers
computing

conclude
concluded
concludes
concluding
conclusion
conclusions
conclusive
conclusively
inconclusive
inconclusively

conduct
conducted
conducting
conducts

consequent
consequence

consequences
consequently

construct
constructed
constructing
construction
constructions
constructive
constructs
reconstruct
reconstructed
reconstructing
reconstruction
reconstructs

consume
consumed
consumer
consumers
consumes
consuming
consumption

credit
credited
crediting
creditor
creditors
credits

culture
cultural
culturally
cultured
cultures
uncultured

design
designed
designer
designers
designing
designs

distinct
distinction
distinctions
distinctive
distinctively
distinctly
indistinct
indistinctly

element
elements

equate
equated
equates
equating
equation
equations

evaluate
evaluated
evaluates
evaluating
evaluation
evaluations
evaluative
re-evaluate
re-evaluated
re-evaluates
re-evaluating
re-evaluation

feature
featured
features
featuring

final
finalise
finalised
finalises
finalising
finalize
finalized
finalizes
finalizing
finality
finally
finals

focus
focused
focuses
focusing
focussed
focusses
focussing
refocus
refocused
refocuses
refocusing
refocussed
refocusses
refocussing

impact
impacted
impacting
impacts

injure
injured
injures
injuries
injuring
injury
uninjured

institute
instituted
institutes
instituting
institution
institutional
institutionalise
institutionalised
institutionalises
institutionalising
institutionalize
institutionalized
institutionalizes
institutionalizing
institutionally
institutions

invest
invested
investing
investment
investments
investor
investors
invests
reinvest
reinvested
reinvesting
reinvestment
reinvests

item
itemisation
itemise
itemised
itemises
itemising
itemization
itemize
itemized
itemizes
itemizing
items

journal
journals

maintain
maintained
maintaining
maintains
maintenance

normal
abnormal
abnormally
normalisation
normalise
normalised
normalises
normalising
normalization
normalize
normalized
normalizes
normalizing
normality
normally

obtain
obtainable
obtained
obtaining
obtains
unobtainable

participate
participant
participants
participated
participates
participating
participation
participatory

perceive
perceived
perceives
perceiving
perception
perceptions

positive
positively

potential
potentially

previous
previously

primary
primarily

purchase
purchased
purchaser
purchasers
purchases
purchasing

range
ranged
ranges
ranging

region
regional
regionally
regions

regulate
deregulated
deregulates
deregulating
deregulation
regulated
regulates
regulating
regulation
regulations
regulator
regulators
regulatory
unregulated

relevant
irrelevance
irrelevant
relevance

reside
resided
residence
resident
residential
residents
resides
residing

resource
resourced
resourceful
resources
resourcing
unresourceful
under-resourced

restrict
restricted
restricting
restriction
restrictions
restrictive
restrictively
restricts
unrestricted
unrestrictive

secure
insecure
insecurities
insecurity
secured
securely
secures
securing
securities
security

seek
seeking
seeks
sought

select
selected
selecting
selection
selections
selective
selectively
selector
selectors
selects

site
sites

strategy
strategic
strategies
strategically
strategist
strategists

survey
surveyed
surveying
surveys

text
texts
textual

tradition
non-traditional
traditional
traditionalist
traditionally
traditions

transfer
transferable
transference
transferred
transferring
transfers

Sublist 3

alternative
alternatively
alternatives

circumstance
circumstances

comment
commentaries
commentary
commentator
commentators
commented
commenting
comments

compensate
compensated
compensates
compensating
compensation
compensations
compensatory

component
componentry
components

consent
consensus
consented
consenting
consents

considerable
considerably

constant
constancy
constantly
constants
inconstancy
inconstantly

constrain
constrained
constraining
constrains
constraint
constraints
unconstrained

contribute
contributed
contributes

contributing
contribution
contributions
contributor
contributors

convene
convention
convenes
convened
convening
conventional
conventionally
conventions
unconventional

coordinate
coordinated
coordinates
coordinating
coordination
coordinator
coordinators
co-ordinate
co-ordinated
co-ordinates
co-ordinating
co-ordination
co-ordinator
co-ordinators

core
cores
coring
cored

corporate
corporates
corporation
corporations

correspond
corresponded
correspondence
corresponding
correspondingly
corresponds

criteria
criterion

deduce
deduced
deduces
deducing
deduction

deductions

demonstrate
demonstrable
demonstrably
demonstrated
demonstrates
demonstrating
demonstration
demonstrations
demonstrative
demonstratively
demonstrator
demonstrators

document
documentation
documented
documenting
documents

dominate
dominance
dominant
dominated
dominates
dominating
domination

emphasis
emphasise
emphasised
emphasising
emphasize
emphasized
emphasizes
emphasizing
emphatic
emphatically

ensure
ensured
ensures
ensuring

exclude
excluded
excludes
excluding
exclusion
exclusionary
exclusionist
exclusions
exclusive
exclusively

framework
frameworks

fund
funded
funder
funders
funding
funds

illustrate
illustrated
illustrates
illustrating
illustration
illustrations
illustrative

immigrate
immigrant
immigrants
immigrated
immigrates
immigrating
immigration

imply
implied
implies
implying

initial
initially

instance
instances

interact
interacted
interacting
interaction
interactions
interactive
interactively
interacts

justify
justifiable
justifiably
justification
justifications
justified
justifies
justifying
unjustified

layer
layered
layering
layers

link
linkage
linkages
linked
linking
links

locate
located
locating
location
locations
relocate
relocated
relocates
relocating
relocation

maximise
max
maximised
maximises
maximising
maximisation
maximize
maximized
maximizes
maximizing
maximization
maximum

minor
minorities
minority
minors

negate
negative
negated
negates
negating
negatively
negatives

outcome
outcomes

partner
partners
partnership
partnerships

philosophy
philosopher
philosophers
philosophical
philosophically
philosophies
philosophise
philosophised
philosophises
philosophising
philosophize
philosophized
philosophizes
philosophizing

physical
physically

proportion
disproportion
disproportionate
disproportionately
proportional
proportionally
proportionate
proportionately
proportions

publish
published
publisher
publishers
publishes
publishing
unpublished

react
reacted
reacts
reacting
reaction
reactionaries
reactionary
reactions
reactive
reactivate
reactivation
reactor
reactors

register
deregister
deregistered
deregistering
deregisters
deregistration
registered

registering
registers
registration

rely
reliability
reliable
reliably
reliance
reliant
relied
relies
relying
unreliable

remove
removable
removal
removals
removed
removes
removing

scheme
schematic
schematically
schemed
schemes
scheming

sequence
sequenced
sequences
sequencing
sequential
sequentially

sex
sexes
sexism
sexual
sexuality
sexually

shift
shifted
shifting
shifts

specify
specifiable
specified
specifies
specifying
unspecified

sufficient
sufficiency
insufficient
insufficiently
sufficiently

task
tasks

technical
technically

technique
techniques

technology
technological
technologically

valid
invalidate
invalidity
validate
validated
validating
validation
validity
validly

volume
volumes
vol

Sublist 4

access
accessed
accesses
accessibility
accessible
accessing
inaccessible

adequate
adequacy
adequately
inadequacies
inadequacy
inadequate
inadequately

annual
annually

apparent
apparently

approximate
approximated
approximately
approximates
approximating
approximation
approximations

attitude
attitudes

attribute
attributable
attributed
attributes
attributing
attribution

civil

code
coded
codes
coding

commit
commitment
commitments
commits
committed
committing

communicate
communicable
communicated
communicates
communicating
communication
communications
communicative
communicatively
uncommunicative

concentrate
concentrated
concentrates
concentrating
concentration

confer
conference
conferences
conferred
conferring
confers

contrast
contrasted
contrasting
contrastive
contrasts

cycle
cycled
cycles
cyclic
cyclical
cycling

debate
debatable
debated
debates
debating

despite

dimension
dimensional
dimensions
multidimensional

domestic
domestically
domesticate
domesticated
domesticating

domestics

emerge
emerged
emergence
emergent
emerges
emerging

error
erroneous
erroneously
errors

ethnic
ethnicity

goal
goals

grant
granted
granting
grants

hence

hypothesis
hypotheses
hypothesise
hypothesised
hypothesises
hypothesising
hypothesize
hypothesized
hypothesizes
hypothesizing
hypothetical
hypothetically

implement
implementation
implemented
implementing
implements

implicate
implicated
implicates
implicating
implication
implications

impose
imposed

imposes
imposing
imposition

integrate
integrated
integrates
integrating
integration

internal
internalise
internalised
internalises
internalising
internalize
internalized
internalizes
internalizing
internally

investigate
investigated
investigates
investigating
investigation
investigations
investigative
investigator
investigators

job
jobs

label
labeled
labeling
labelled
labelling
labels

mechanism
mechanisms

obvious
obviously

occupy
occupancy
occupant
occupants
occupation
occupational
occupations
occupied

occupier
occupiers
occupies
occupying

option
optional
options

output
outputs

overall

parallel
paralleled
parallelled
paralleling
parallelling
parallels
unparalleled
unparaleled

parameter
parameters

phase
phased
phases
phasing

predict
predictability
predictable

predictably
predicted
predicting
prediction
predictions
predicts
unpredictability
unpredictable

principal
principally

prior

professional
professionally
professionals
professionalism

project
projected
projecting
projection
projections
projects

promote
promoted
promoter
promoters
promotes
promoting
promotion
promotions

regime
regimes

resolve
resolution
resolved
resolves
resolving
unresolved

retain
retained
retaining
retainer
retainers
retains
retention
retentive

series

statistic
statistician
statisticians
statistical
statistically
statistics

status

stress
stressed
stresses
stressful

stressing
unstressed

subsequent
subsequently

sum
summation
summed
summing
sums

summary
summaries
summarise
summarised
summarises
summarising
summarisation
summarisations
summarization
summarizations
summarize
summarized
summarizes
summarizing

undertake
undertaken
undertakes
undertaking
undertook

Sublist 5

academy
academia
academic
academically
academics
academies

adjust
adjusted
adjusting
adjustment
adjustments
adjusts
readjust
readjusted
readjusting
readjustment
readjustments
readjusts

alter
alterable
alteration
alterations
altered
altering
alternate
alternating
alters
unalterable
unaltered

amend
amended
amending
amendment
amendments
amends

aware
awareness
unaware

capacity
capacities
incapacitate
incapacitated

challenge
challenged
challenger
challengers
challenges
challenging

clause
clauses

compound
compounded
compounding
compounds

conflict
conflicted
conflicting
conflicts

consult
consultancy
consultant
consultants
consultation
consultations
consultative
consulted
consults
consulting

contact
contactable
contacted
contacting
contacts

decline
declined
declines
declining

discrete
discretely
discretion
discretionary
indiscrete
indiscretion

draft
drafted
drafting
drafts
redraft
redrafted
redrafting
redrafts

enable
enabled
enables
enabling

energy
energetic
energetically
energies

enforce
enforced
enforcement
enforces
enforcing

entity
entities

equivalent
equivalence

evolve
evolution
evolved
evolving
evolves
evolutionary
evolutionist
evolutionists

expand
expanded
expanding
expands
expansion
expansionism
expansive

expose
exposed
exposes
exposing
exposure
exposures

external
externalisation
externalise
externalised
externalises
externalising
externality
externalization
externalize
externalized
externalizes
externalizing
externally

facilitate
facilitated
facilitates
facilities
facilitating
facilitation
facilitator
facilitators
facility

fundamental
fundamentally

generate
generated
generates
generating

generation
generations

image
imagery
images

liberal
liberalise
liberalism
liberalisation
liberalised
liberalises
liberalising
liberalization
liberalize
liberalized
liberalizes
liberalizing
liberate
liberated
liberates
liberation
liberations
liberating
liberator
liberators
liberally
liberals

licence
licences
license
licensed
licensing
licenses
unlicensed

logic
illogical
illogically
logical
logically
logician
logicians

margin
marginal
marginally
margins

medical
medically

mental
mentality
mentally

modify
modification
modifications
modified
modifies
modifying
unmodified

monitor
monitored
monitoring
monitors
unmonitored

network
networked
networking
networks

notion
notions

objective
objectively
objectivity

orient
orientate
orientated
orientates
orientation
orientating
oriented
orienting
orients
reorient
reorientation

perspective
perspectives

precise
imprecise
precisely
precision

prime
primacy

psychology
psychological
psychologically
psychologist
psychologists

pursue
pursued
pursues
pursuing
pursuit
pursuits

ratio
ratios

reject
rejected
rejecting
rejection
rejects
rejections

revenue
revenues

stable
instability
stabilisation
stabilise
stabilised
stabilises
stabilising
stabilization
stabilize
stabilized
stabilizes
stabilizing
stability
unstable

style
styled
styles
styling
stylish
stylise
stylised
stylises
stylising
stylize
stylized
stylizes
stylizing

substitute
substituted
substitutes
substituting
substitution

sustain
sustainable
sustainability
sustained
sustaining
sustains
sustenance
unsustainable

symbol
symbolic
symbolically
symbolise
symbolises
symbolised
symbolising
symbolism
symbolize
symbolized
symbolizes
symbolizing
symbols

target
targeted
targeting
targets

transit
transited
transiting
transition
transitional
transitions
transitory
transits

trend
trends

version
versions

welfare

whereas

This achievement test will help you:
- check your knowledge of these words;
- check the progress you have made in understanding these words.

There is no time limit for this test. The point of the test is to allow you to see how much you have learnt by studying this book, and to give you an idea of what you need to look at again.

All the words and sentences in this test are taken from Units 6 to 10.

We suggest you complete the test and then check the answers at the back of the book. If you make any mistakes you can go back and look at Units 6 to 10.

Task 1: Meanings of words

Complete the pairs of sentences below with a word from the box. In each pair you need the same word for both sentences. In the case of verbs, a different ending may be needed, e.g., ~*s*, ~*ed*, ~*ing*. In the case of nouns you have to decide whether the singular or plural form is appropriate.

dominant	~~available~~	restrict	apparent	aware	vary

Example:

Information about this product is freely ___*available*___ on the Internet.

Updates are ___*available*___ from our website.

1 Distances from the accommodation to the university _____ from two to six kilometres.

   Journey times may _____ slightly, depending on the time of day.

2 Many countries have _____ smoking in public places such as bars and restaurants.

   Smoking is _____ to designated areas.

3 The company is trying to maintain its _____ position in the market.

   Ten years ago the company enjoyed a _____ share of the market.

4 It was soon _____ that there was a serious problem with the equipment.

   The flight was cancelled for no _____ reason

5 Few people are _____ of the dangers a sudden change in air pressure can cause.

   He suddenly became _____ of someone following him.

Task 2: Multi-meaning words

In this exercise you are given three definitions for the bold words in the sentences. Choose the correct meaning of the bold words according to the context in which they appear.

Example:
It doesn't matter which **order** you answer the questions in.

a) the way that things or events are arranged in relation to each other, for example showing whether something is first, second, third, etc.

b) an instruction to do something that is given by someone in authority

c) a request for food or drink in a restaurant or bar

Answer: a) the way that things or events are arranged in relation to each other, for example showing whether something is first, second, third, etc.

1 Perhaps the most obvious sign of globalisation is in the economic **area**.

   a) a particular part of a city, town, region or country

   b) the amount of space covered by the surface of a place or shape

   c) a particular subject or range of activities

2 Developed countries **consume** huge quantities of raw materials.

   a) to use time, energy, goods, etc.

   b) to eat or drink something

   c) to destroy something

3 A number of different human activities have **contributed** to climate change.

   a) to give money, goods, ideas or time and effort

   b) to be one of the things that make something happen

   c) to write stories, articles, features, etc., for a newspaper or magazine

4 Regular exercise **promotes** good health and normal sleep patterns.

   a) to help something to increase or develop

   b) to move someone to a better, more responsible job in a company

   c) to encourage people to support or use something

5 Many companies today are operating on extremely tight **margins**.

   a) the empty space at the side of a page

   b) the difference in the number of points between the winners and the losers of a sports event or competition

   c) the difference between what it costs to buy or produce something and its selling price

Task 3: Word classes

Look at the sentences. Decide what word class would fill each gap. Write *v* (verb), *n* (noun), *adj* (adjective) or *adv* (adverb) in the brackets after each gap.

Example:

The university should _____ (_v_) more facilities for disabled students.

1 The government's policy is to allow banks to _____ (__) independently, free of external controls

2 Many people do not feel _____ (__) as a result of the sharp rise in crime.

3 A high _____ (__) of babies born to mothers who were smokers have a less than average body weight at birth.

4 They see education as the first _____ (__) in the battle to improve public health in this region.

5 Interest based on the amount of money originally invested and the interest already earned is known as _____ (__) interest.

Task 4: Word families

4.1   Choose the correct form of the word in brackets to complete the following sentences. In the case of verbs a different ending may be needed, e.g., ~ed, ~ing, ~s.

Example:

The average daily food __requirement__ for an adult is between 2000 and 3000 calories. (require)

a) The most recent _____ of the research suggests that human activities have had an influence on the global climate. (assess)

b) Contrary to popular _____, vigorous exercise is not necessarily good for your health. (perceive)

c) Focusing on research and development will have _____ for short-term profitability. (imply)

d) The rise of budget airlines in Europe has meant that cheap air travel is now _____ to almost everyone in the European Union. (access)

e) It is _____ impossible to include all the students at the university in the survey. (logic)

Word families and lexical cohesion

4.2   Complete the pairs of sentences below by filling both the gaps with the correct form of the word that appears in brackets at the end of each sentence.

Example:

It is often difficult to ____adjust____ to a change of career. Some people fail to make the ___adjustment___ and simply go back to their old job. (adjust)

a) The plan has been drawn up in _____ with our Far Eastern partners. We attempted to _____ them at all stages of the project. (consult)

b) Living standards in the area are _____ rapidly. The main reason for this _____ is the continuing armed conflict in the region. (decline)

c) The US government claims that the weapons their planes use are very _____. The number of civilian casualties on the ground would suggest that this _____ is more theoretical than real. (precise)

d) _____ in the exchange rate is a requirement for continued growth. A _____ currency will encourage investment. (stable)

Task 5: Prefixes

Complete the following sentences using either:

- the word in brackets; or
- a prefix from the list below + the word in brackets.

In the case of verbs a different ending may be needed, e.g., ~ed, ~ing, ~s.

| re~ | in~ | un~ | mis~ | over~ | under~ |

Example:

Old cars are very often _uneconomical_ . (economical)

1 Compared with the problems people in the Third World have with diseases, our worries are _____. (significant)

2 The patient received serious injuries in the accident but her vital organs were _____. (affected)

3 Statistics can sometimes be _____ and lead to over-generalised conclusions. (reliable)

4 Countries like Canada are planning to _____ almost 100 percent of their waste. (cycle)

5 Her instructions were both complicated and _____ with the result that I was late for the meeting. (precise)

Task 6: Collocations

Using your knowledge of collocation and paying particular attention to the bold words, complete the gaps in these sentences.

The word class you need is given in brackets at the end of each sentence. In the case of verbs a different ending may be needed, e.g., ~ed, ~ing, ~s.

Example:

Recent **studies** show that women still earn less than men for doing the same job. (adjective)

She was delighted to _have_ the **opportunity** to talk to someone who shared her interest in classical music. (verb)

1 There is little or no scientific _____ to **support** this **theory**. (noun)

2 Changes in energy policy will **have** a **huge** _____ on the environment. (noun)

3 The government is _____ the relief **effort** as numerous aid agencies arrive in the affected area. (verb)

4 The findings **confirmed** the _____ that smokers are at greater risk of heart attack. (noun)

5 The local economy **expanded** _____ during the 1980s and 1990s but is currently in a period of crisis. (adverb)

Task 7: Word Grammar

Discovering noun patterns

7.1 Look at the nouns in bold in the sentences below and identify:

- which nouns are followed by prepositions;
- which nouns are followed by "*that* + clause";
- which nouns are followed by "*to* + infinitive".

a) There is clear **evidence** of a link between price reductions and increased sales.

b) The test measures children's **achievements** in different sports.

c) This particular treatment is offered as an **alternative** to invasive surgery.

d) Many people take the **attitude** that people over 60 years of age no longer useful to society.

e) The government is concerned about its **capacity** to invest in the country's infrastructure.

Transitive and intransitive verbs

7.2 The verbs in the sentences below are sometimes transitive and sometimes intransitive. Look at the verbs as they are used in these sentences and decide if they are transitive (VT) or intransitive (VI).

a) Waiting times **vary** and may be up to two months.

b) The research project will **focus** on social problems in the city.

c) Owners had until the end of 1990 to **register** their weapons.

d) A lot of money has been **committed** to the reconstruction of the city.

e) She **declined** the offer.

Now check your answers in the key on page 195

Answer key

Unit 1: Multi-meaning words

Task 1
Exercise 1.1

1	a)	**6**	b)
2	b)	**7**	c)
3	a)	**8**	b)
4	a)	**9**	c)
5	b)	**10**	a)

Exercise 1.2

1	a)	**6**	b)
2	b)	**7**	c)
3	b)	**8**	b)
4	b)	**9**	b)
5	a)	**10**	b)

Task 2
Exercise 2.1

1	b)	**6**	b)
2	b)	**7**	a)
3	a)	**8**	a)
4	b)	**9**	b)
5	a)	**10**	b)

Exercise 2.2
Example definitions:
a) subject (noun): *an idea, topic, problem or situation that you discuss in speech or writing*
b) heated (adjective): *impassioned or highly emotional. Full of angry and excited feelings.*
c) perform (verb): *to work or do something (well, badly)*
d) concern (noun): *a feeling of worry, especially about something such as a social problem, etc.*
e) far (adjective): *to a great degree*

Task 3
Exercise 3.1
a) noun, verb
b) noun, verb
c) noun, verb, adjective
d) noun, verb, adjective, adverb
e) noun, verb
f) noun, verb
g) noun, adjective
h) noun, verb
i) noun, verb

Unit 2: Word classes – nouns, verbs, adverbs and adjectives

Task 1
Exercise 1.1
Nouns: study, tests, Mathematics, classes, contrast, class
Verbs: ranks, have slipped, average
Adjectives: developed, American, advanced, large, normal
Adverbs: particularly

Task 2
Exercise 2.1

Word	Word class
entire	*adjective*
basically	*adverb*
avoid	*verb*
existence	*noun*
discover	*verb*
regular	*adjective, noun*
relatively	*adverb*
provide	*verb*
prevent	*verb*
highly	*adverb*
security	*noun*

Exercise 2.2

a)	adverb	**g)**	verb
b)	adjective	**h)**	noun
c)	noun	**i)**	adverb
d)	verb	**j)**	adjective
e)	verb	**k)**	verb
f)	adverb		

Exercise 2.3

a) relatively   **g)** avoid
b) entire   **h)** existence
c) security   **i)** highly
d) discovered   **j)** regular
e) prevent   **k)** provide
f) basically

Task 3
Exercise 3.1

Word	Word class
stem	*noun, verb*
match	*noun, verb*
influence	*noun, verb*
lack	*noun, verb*
rank	*noun, verb, adjective*
spare	*noun, verb, adjective*
joint	*noun, adjective*
risk	*noun, verb*
sample	*noun, verb, adjective*

Exercise 3.2

a) adjective   **f)** verb
b) noun   **g)** verb
c) verb   **h)** noun
d) verb   **i)** noun
e) adjective

Exercise 3.3

Word	Word class
experience	*noun, verb*
rates	*noun, verb*
double	*noun, verb, adjective, adverb*
essential	*noun, adjective*
support	*noun, verb*
ideal	*noun, verb, adjective*
border	*noun, verb, adjective*
prompt	*noun, verb, adjective*
blame	*noun, verb*

Exercise 3.4

a) verb   **f)** adjective
b) verb   **g)** noun
c) verb   **h)** adverb
d) adjective   **i)** verb
e) verb

Task 4
Exercise 4.1

1
a) adjective   **c)** noun
b) verb   **d)** adverb

2
a) noun and verb   **c)** adjective and noun
b) noun and verb   **d)** noun and verb

Exercise 4.2

Knowledge of word class helps understanding of how to use <u>words</u> effectively. The best way to understand what word class a word <u>belongs</u> to is to read it in the context of a <u>sentence</u> or a paragraph. It is helpful to know that some words can belong to two or <u>more</u> word classes, for example, *prompt* can be a noun, a <u>verb</u> or an adjective, and *spare* can be a <u>noun</u>, a verb or an adjective.

Unit 3: Word families and word parts

Task 1
Exercise 1.1

Verb	Same form or different?
change	-
restrict	*restriction*
employ	*employment*
cause	-
offer	-
depend	*dependence*
claim	-
decrease	-
respond	*response*
influence	-
suggest	*suggestion*
aim	-
argue	*argument*
risk	-
waste	-

Task 2
Exercise 2.1

Nouns: behaviour, development, difference, equality, formation
Verbs: realise, activate, calculate
Adjectives: appropriate, economical, social
Adverbs: gradually

Exercise 2.2

Nouns: ~ion, ~ment, ~our, ~ence, ~ity, ~ness
Verbs: ~ise, ~ate
Adjectives: ~al, ~ate, ~ive
Adverbs: ~ly

Task 3

Exercise 3.1

Prefixes	Example words
re~	rearrange, reboot
inter~	interpersonal, international
anti~	anticlimax, anticlockwise
geo~	geopolitics, geophysics
post~	postmodern, postgraduate
micro~	microclimate, microorganism
semi~	semidetached, semifinal
sub~	substandard, subconscious
thermo~	thermometer

Exercise 3.2

a) post
b) semi
c) thermo
d) micro
e) inter
f) sub
g) geo
h) anti
i) bi
j) mono

Task 4

Exercise 4.1

a) unsatisfactory
b) inefficient
c) unlikely
d) disappearance
e) unprincipled
f) abnormal
g) irrelevant
h) illegal
i) immoral
j) unpublished

Task 5

Exercise 5.1

long – length
need – necessary
obey – obedience
poor – poverty
loan – lend
space – spatial
describe – description

Task 6

Exercise 6.1

Nouns: competition, decision, permission, permit, economy, origin, complication, absence, certainty
Verbs: compete, decide, permit, economise, originate, complicate,
Adjectives: competitive, decisive, economic, economical, complicated, absent, certain
Adverbs: decisively, economically, originally, certainly

Exercise 6.2

a) certainty
b) absence
c) economically
d) original
e) decision
f) permission
g) complications

Task 7

Exercise 7.1

a) explained/explanation
b) different/differences
c) argument/argue
d) difficult/difficulty
e) develop/development

Task 8

Exercise 8.1

a) centenary, percentage, century
b) transport, portable, import, export
c) biology, psychology, geology
d) television, telephone, telescope
e) visual, vision, visible
f) prospect, respect, perspective, spectator
g) photograph, telephoto, photosynthesis

Exercise 8.2

a) photo
b) tele
c) port
d) spect
e) cent
f) vis
g) ology

Task 9

Exercise 9.1

a) compete: *competition, competitive, competitor*
b) compare: *comparison, comparative, compared*
c) direct: *direction, director, directed, misdirect*
d) prepare: *preparation, prepared, unprepared*
e) depend: *dependence, depending, dependant, independent*
(Sentences depend on students)

Unit 4: Collocations

Task 1

Exercise 1.1

1

a) introduce
b) observe
c) present

2
a) developmental
b) ingenious
c) young
d) basic

Task 2
Exercise 2.1
a) to put, to be, to come under, to have, to express, to take
b) on, about, over, for
c) *to* + infinitive

Exercise 2.2
doubt
have no doubts about
express doubts over
there are doubts about

pressure
put pressure on
there is pressure on
come under pressure to

opportunity
have the opportunity to
there are opportunities for
take an opportunity to

Exercise 2.3
a) for
b) are
c) puts
d) on
e) is
f) have

Task 3
Exercise 3.1
a) do, mean, have, be in, run
b) make, put in, be
c) make, have, cause
d) make, see, have, be (is)
e) achieve, have, produce
f) be (is), give, establish
g) be (is), bridge, fill, see, leave, find
h) lower, achieve, conform to, set,
i) give, cause, have, show, create, express, voice

Task 4
Exercise 4.1
a) between
b) on
c) over
d) on
e) between
f) with

Task 5
Exercise 5.1
a) big, important, significant, major, serious, minor, slight, fundamental
b) large, short, regular, medical, steady, constant, endless, limited
c) high, low, normal, strict, moral

Exercise 5.2
a) main
b) sole
c) particular
d) growing
e) huge
f) recent
g) practical
h) human
i) growing, public
j) greater

Task 6
Exercise 6.1
a) effectively
b) significantly
c) especially
d) clearly
e) gradually
f) particularly
g) increasingly
h) relatively
i) probably
j) rapidly
k) strongly
l) comparatively

a) significantly: significantly reduce
gradually: gradually decreases
probably: (was) probably caused
rapidly: spread rapidly
strongly: strongly disagreed

b) important: especially important
particularly: particularly useful
increasingly: increasingly difficult
relatively: relatively recent
comparatively: comparatively easy

Task 7
Exercise 7.1
a) *have* trouble
have an effect
manage resources
see a connection

b) have trouble *with*
have an impact *on*
do business *with*

c) widening *gap*
sole *purpose*
growing *demand*

d) *reduce* significantly
spread rapidly
stated clearly

e) *increasingly* difficult
especially important
particularly useful

Unit 5: Word grammar

Task 1
Exercise 1.1
a) years after the discovery
   migrants from Europe
   dangers of migration
   passage to North America
b) a year's wages
c) farm labourer

Task 2
Exercise 2.1

Noun	*that* + clause	Not followed by *that* + clause
belief	✓	
notion	✓	
theory	✓	
view	✓	
idea	✓	
fact	✓	
suggestion	✓	

Task 3
Exercise 3.1

a) 2
b) 2
c) 1; 1
d) 1
e) 4
f) 1
g) 1
h) 1
i) 1
j) 1; 1
k) 2;1

Exercise 3.2

c) of; of
d) of
f) for
g) of
h) of
i) on
j) on; of
k) that; of

Exercise 3.3

a) 1
b) 3
c) 2
d) 2
e) 1
f) 1
g) 3
h) 3
i) 3
j) 1
k) 2
l) 3

Exercise 3.4

a) to
e) of
f) of
j) to

Task 4
Exercise 4.1
a) **market** leader, town, research, price
b) **computer** technology, system, game, age
c) weight **problem**
d) insurance, **company** car, policy, director, employee
e) government, father, mother, authority, unemployment **figure/figures**
f) business, exchange, tax, success, failure **rate**

Task 5
Exercise 5.1

a) 3
b) 2
c) 2
d) 3
e) 3
f) 1
g) 1
h) 3
i) 2
j) 1

Exercise 5.2
a) for
d) for
e) for
h) to

Exercise 5.3
necessary, difficult, possible, clear, likely

Exercise 5.4
a) common, customary, useful
b) common, certain, customary, useful
c) certain
d) common, certain, customary, bound, useful

Task 7
Exercise 7.1
a) intransitive
b) transitive
c) transitive
d) transitive
e) transitive
f) transitive
g) transitive
h) transitive
i) transitive

Exercise 7.3
Transitive: present, include, suggest, describe, lack, mention
Intransitive: appear, rise, remain, exist, result, belong, interfere

Exercise 7.4
a) to
b) with

Exercise 7.4

a) VI	**e)** VT
b) VI	**f)** VT
c) VI	**g)** VT
d) VT	

Task 8
Exercise 8.1

Verb	*that* + clause	Not followed by *that* + clause
decrease		✓
behave		✓
state	✓	
consider	✓	
admit	✓	
introduce		✓

Exercise 8.2
b) (was) agreed
c) suggests
d) (is worth) mentioning
e) claim
f) (have) discovered
g) (have come to) accept
i) admitted

Task 9
Exercise 9.1

Verbs	wh~ word
doubt	*whether, what*
consider	*whether, what, which, when, why*
determine	*whether, what, which, when, why*
explain	*whether, what, when, why*
decide	*whether, what, which, when, why*
describe	*whether, what, which, when, why*
realise	*whether, what, which, when, why*
discuss	*whether, what, which, when, why*

Exercise 9.3
a) We need to discuss what kind of strategy we want for next year.
b) They doubted whether the document had ever existed.
c) I will also describe why I still find it difficult to accept his explanation.
d) We are considering whether we should update our advice to visitors.
e) People have a right to decide what they should do with their own money.

Task 10
Exercise 10.1
a) show, argue, suggest
b) explain, ask, discover
c) evidence, suggestion, answer
d) clear, possible, likely
e) customary, common, useful

Unit 6: Academic Word List – Sublist 1

Task 1
Exercise 1.1
vary – to change or be different in different circumstances
proceed – to carry on doing something that has already started
approach – a way of dealing with a situation or problem
occur – to happen
evident – easy to see, notice, or understand
assume – to accept something as true, although you do not have proof and no one has told you it is true
respond – to say or do something in reaction to something else
factor – one of the things that causes a situation or influence the way it happens
available – able to be found, bought or obtained
interpret – to take actions or behaviours as having a particular meaning
derive – to obtain or come from another source

Exercise 1.2

a) assume	**f)** factors
b) vary	**g)** occur
c) evident	**h)** requires
d) interpret	**i)** proceed
e) approach	

Task 2
Exercise 2.1

1 b)	**6** b)
2 c)	**7** a)
3 a)	**8** c)
4 b)	**9** c)
5 b)	**10** c)

Task 3
Exercise 3.1

Word	Word class
benefit	*verb, noun*
research	*verb, noun*
policy	*noun*
individual	*noun, adjective*
function	*verb, noun*
assess	*verb*
specific	*adjective*
finance	*verb, noun*
consist of/in	*verb*
identify	*verb*

Exercise 3.2
a) verb **f)** adjective
b) adjective **g)** verb
c) noun **h)** noun
d) noun **i)** verb
e) verb **j)** verb

Exercise 3.3
a) benefit **f)** specific
b) individual **g)** identify
c) research **h)** finance
d) policy **i)** function
e) assess **j)** consists

Task 4
Exercise 4.1
Nouns: assessment, economy, variation, variable, analysis, significance, indication, response, environment, creation, interpretation, definition
Verbs: assess, vary, analyse, indicate, respond, create, define
Adjectives: economic, economical, variable, significant, indicative, responsive, creative
Adverbs: economically, significantly, environmentally

Exercise 4.2
a) significant **f)** analysis
b) variations **g)** assessment
c) interpreted **h)** indicate
d) create **i)** responded
e) definition **j)** environmental

Task 5
Exercise 5.1
a) insignificant
b) unavailable
c) recreate
d) uneconomical
e) misinterpret
f) unresponsive
g) reassess
h) inconsistent
i) over/underestimate

Exercise 5.2
a) occur **e)** responsive
b) unavailable **f)** misinterpreted
c) inconsistent **g)** reassess
d) insignificant **h)** underestimated

Task 6
Exercise 6.1
interpret data
meet requirements
carry out research
adopt a policy
identify the person
assess effects

Exercise 6.2
a) play **e)** estimate
b) define **f)** assess
c) adopt **g)** create
d) establish

Exercise 6.3
a) issues **d)** an analysis
b) methods **e)** benefit
c) theory

Exercise 6.4
a) (is) needed **h)** to support
b) (has) shown **i)** provide
c) shows **j)** examining
d) provides **k)** (have) used
e) obtain **l)** adopt
f) show **m)** claim
g) involves **n)** (has) brought

Task 7

Exercise 7.1

- what prepositions are used after the nouns

b) of **l)** to
d) about **m)** in
e) of **n)** to
f) for **o)** from
h) of **p)** of
i) of **q)** of
j) of **r)** on
k) to

- which nouns are followed by "*that* + clause"

a) theory
c) assumption
g) evidence

- which "noun + noun" combinations are used

r) *Government* policy

Exercise 7.2

a) government; team
b) analysis; collection
c) collection; decision-making; production

Exercise 7.3

a) costs; shortages; force; market; movement; manual
b) social; housing; child; unemployment; concert
c) market; industry; licence; price
d) code; key; surface

Exercise 7.4

Transitive verbs: assume, create, distribute, finance, involve, issue, process
Intransitive verbs: proceed, function, legislate, occur

Exercise 7.5

Answers depend on dictionary used.

Exercise 7.6

Answers depend on dictionary used.

Exercise 7.7

a) VI **d)** VI
b) VT **e)** VT
c) VI **f)** VI

Exercise 7.8

a) require – VT **f)** have identified – VT
b) varies – VI **g)** to establish – VT
c) indicates – VT **h)** include – VT
d) define – VT **i)** involving – VT
e) is proceeding – VI

Task 8

Exercise 8.1

a) school examinations
ocean temperature
greenhouse gas
oil prices
government policy
b) approach
source
factor
process
research
c) approach
contract
focus
permit
benefit

Unit 7: Academic Word List – Sublist 2

Task 1

Exercise 1.1

appropriate – right for a specific use
equate – to treat two things as equal or the same
distinct – obviously different or part of a contradictory type
potential – the possibilities that something or someone has to offer
feature – one of many parts of an idea or situation
restrict – to ensure something stays within a limit or limits
aspect – a part of something that stands out as being important or interesting
complex – made up of multiple parts and often complicated
consequent – the natural outcome that follows from a specific situation

Exercise 1.2

a) distinct **f)** equate
b) feature **g)** restricted
c) complex **h)** potential
d) appropriate **i)** aspects
e) consequent

Task 2

Exercise 2.1

1 b) **6** a)
2 a) **7** c)
3 c) **8** a)
4 a) **9** a)
5 c)

Task 3

Exercise 3.1

Word	Word class
acquire	*verb*
community	*noun*
relevant	*adjective*
potential	*noun, adjective*
resource	*verb, noun*
transfer	*verb, noun*
focus	*verb, noun*
previous	*adjective*
secure	*verb, adjective*

Exercise 3.2

a) adjective
b) verb
c) adjective
d) noun
e) noun
f) adjective
g) adjective
h) verb
i) noun

Exercise 3.3

a) previous
b) concluded
c) potential
d) resources
e) transfer
f) relevant
g) secure
h) acquire
i) community

Task 4

Exercise 4.1

Nouns: achievement, normality, participant, participation, maintenance, perception, regulation, strategy, region, resource, complexity, distinction, computer
Verbs: achieve, participate, maintain, perceive, regulate, select, computerise
Adjectives: normal, strategic, selective, regional, resourceful, complex, distinct
Adverbs: –

Exercise 4.2

a) perception
b) participation
c) achievements
d) strategy
e) consequence
f) maintenance
g) assistance
h) selective
i) regulations

Task 5

Exercise 5.1

a) irrelevant
b) unregulated
c) inappropriate
d) reconstruct
e) unaffected
f) abnormal
g) reinvest
h) unobtainable
i) unrestricted
j) inconclusive

Exercise 5.2

a) Irrelevant
b) unrestricted
c) abnormal
d) unaffected
e) construction
f) regulated
g) reinvest
h) unobtainable
i) inconclusive

Task 6

Exercise 6.1

exploit the potential of something
make a distinction
affect one's health
attract investment
conduct an investigation
restrict access

Exercise 6.2

a) affect
b) maintain
c) perceive
d) consume
e) design
f) transfer
g) evaluate

Exercise 6.3

a) primary
b) positive
c) final
d) normal
e) appropriate

Exercise 6.4

a)
to have (an); to reduce (the)	impact
enforce	regulations
make (a)	distinction
to lift; to impose	restrictions
to have; to face (the)	consequences
to commission (a)	report

b)
aspect(s) of	*life; the problem*
participation in	*the research; elections*
relevant (to)	*to our work*
regulation of	*money markets*
range of	*products; solutions*

c)
vast; wide	range
huge	impact
every; social	aspect(s)
far-reaching	consequences

d) *particularly*   relevant

Task 7
Exercise 7.1
• what prepositions are used after the nouns

a) between
b) of
c) of
e) of
f) on; of
g) in
h) of

i) in
j) by
k) on; of
l) of
m) for
n) of

• which nouns are followed by "that + clause"
d) perception

• which "noun + noun" combinations are used
b) children's achievements

Exercise 7.2
a) computer
b) construction
c) restrictions

Exercise 7.3
a) work; planning; building; health; safety
b) national; state; job; guard; light; risk; service; forces; procedures; firm
c) accounts; course; college

Exercise 7.4
Transitive verbs: credit, feature, finalise, regulate, secure, perceive, select, survey
Intransitive verbs: reside

Exercise 7.5
Answers depend on dictionary used.

Exercise 7.6
Answers depend on dictionary used.

Exercise 7.7
a) VI
b) VI
c) VI

d) VT
e) VI

Task 8
Exercise 8.1
a) distinct forms
complex relationship
primary objective
previous resident
irrelevant information
b) feature writer
mineral resources
children's achievement
voter participation
computer system

c) credit for
aspect of
distinction between
consequence of
impact on

Unit 8: Academic Word List – Sublist 3

Task 1
Exercise 1.1
excluding – not including
core – the strongest members of a group
consent – to allow something to happen
constrain – to prevent something from happening
dominant – stronger or more obvious than other people or things which are similar
initial – happening when something first starts
outcome – the result or consequences of something
layer – one of several levels within an organisation
deduce – to produce an opinion as a result of information

Exercise 1.2
a) outcome
b) dominant
c) consent
d) excluding
e) initial

f) core
g) layer
h) deduced
i) constrained

Task 2
Exercise 2.1

1	b)	**8**	a)
2	b)	**9**	a)
3	a)	**10**	a)
4	a)	**11**	b)
5	a)	**12**	c)
6	b)	**13**	b)
7	a)		

Task 3
Exercise 3.1

Word	Word class
link	noun, verb
proportion	noun, verb
sequence	noun
volume	noun
alternative	noun, adjective
consent	noun, verb
minority	noun
register	noun, verb
specify	verb
comment	noun, verb
emphasise	verb

Exercise 3.2

a) noun   **g)** verb
b) verb   **h)** verb
c) verb   **i)** noun
d) noun   **j)** verb
e) adjective   **k)** verb
f) noun

Exercise 3.3

a) sequence   **g)** comment
b) linked   **h)** specify
c) emphasises   **i)** minorities
d) proportion   **j)** registered
e) alternative   **k)** shifting
f) consent

Task 4

Exercise 4.1

Nouns: reaction, validity, validation, reliance, reliability, illustration, location, justification, implication, compensation, contribution, constraint, deduction, proportion, emphasis
Verbs: react, specify, rely, illustrate, locate, justify, imply, correspond, compensate, contribute, constrain, deduce, emphasise
Adjectives: specific, reliable, initial, alternative, constant, exclusive, proportional, sufficient,
Adverbs: initially, correspondingly, alternatively, constantly, exclusively, sufficiently,

Exercise 4.2

a) emphasis   **f)** sufficiently
b) Initially   **g)** constantly
c) reaction   **h)** alternatively
d) implications   **i)** contribution
e) specific

Task 5

Exercise 5.1

a) insufficient   **e)** relocate
b) unspecified   **f)** unjustified
c) unreliable   **g)** unconventional
d) disproportionate

Exercise 5.2

a) unreliable   **d)** relocate
b) invalidated   **e)** unjustified
c) insufficient

Task 6

Exercise 6.1

a) demonstrate   **f)** predict
b) make   **g)** is
c) coordinating   **h)** justify
d) pay   **i)** maximise
e) given   **j)** follow

Exercise 6.2

a) illustrate
b) shift
c) dominate
d) emphasise
e) exclude

Exercise 6.3

a) illustrate; point
b) emphasises; importance
c) dominate; world
d) shift; attention

Exercise 6.4

initial stage
ethnic minorities
positive outcome
dominant position
constant temperature
different components
alternative ways of coping
valid ideas
full compensation
enormous shift

Exercise 6.5

a) evidence; food; money; means
b) point; place; person; group; detail; thing
c) ticket; document; agreement; reason; argument; criticism
d) person; friend; worker; source; type
e) offence; illness; injury; change; importance; issue

Exercise 6.6

a) *have*   implications
    give; draw up   criteria
    make (a)   contribution

b) *serious*   implications
    certain; exceptional   circumstances
    only; new   criterion
    significant; small   proportion
    first   reaction
    prior   consent
    huge; significant   contribution

c) criterion/criteria   *for*
    framework   *for; with*
    proportion   *of*
    reaction   *to*

d) *under; in*   circumstances
    with; without   consent

Task 7

Exercise 7.1

• what prepositions are used after the nouns

a) to		**i)** of	
d) for		**j)** of	
e) of		**k)** for	
f) on		**m)** to	
g) of		**n)** of	
h) of			

• which nouns are followed by "that + clause"
c) implication

• what prepositions come before *core* and *instance*
at (the) core
in (this) instance

• which noun is followed by "*to* + infinitive"
l) schemes

• which nouns are followed by the verb *to be*
(i.e., *is, are*, etc.) + *to* + infinitive
b) alternative

Exercise 7.2

ozone layer
climate change
repair work
car engine
radio station
metal implements
stock exchange
peer pressure
transport infrastructure

Exercise 7.3

Transitive verbs: imply, ensure, deduce
Intransitive verbs: correspond, interact

Exercise 7.4

Answers depend on dictionary used.

Exercise 7.5

Answers depend on dictionary used.

Exercise 7.6

a) VT	**d)** VT
b) VI	**d)** VT
c) VI	

Exercise 7.7

Answers depend on dictionary used.

Exercise 7.8

a) This story illustrates how important religion is in Middle Eastern culture.
b) This section will attempt to demonstrate how the Stock Exchange operates.
c) Regulations specify how many hours drivers can work.
d) They will be demonstrating how to use the latest software.
e) The contract clearly specifies who is not covered by the agreement.
f) The purpose of this presentation is to illustrate how a small company like this one can increase profits.

Task 8

Exercise 8.1

a) initial performance
   positive outcome
   core audience
   ethnic minorities
   active contribution
b) engine component
   ozone layer
   football management
   governement scheme
   stock exchange
c) outcome
   contribution
   shift
   proportion
   alternative
d) consent
   fund
   shift
   scheme
   link

Unit 9: Academic Word List – Sublist 4

Task 1

Exercise 1.1

overall – including everything or considering something as a whole
impose – to force people to accept something
hence – for this reason or as a result of this
adequate – good enough or sufficient for a specific purpose
prior – happening previous to a particular time
implement – to make something happen that has been officially decided

attribute – to believe that a situation or event is caused by something

integrate – when two or more suitable things are connected work together more effectively than before

apparent – obvious or easy to notice

Exercise 1.2
a) integrated
b) hence
c) impose
d) overall
e) attributed
f) adequate
g) implement
h) prior
i) apparent

Task 2
Exercise 2.1
1 b)
2 a)
3 a)
4 a)
5 b)
6 a)
7 b)
8 a)
9 b)
10 c)

Task 3
Exercise 3.1

Word	Word class
grant	noun, verb
hypothesis	noun
civil	adjective
contrast	noun, verb
cycle	noun, verb
internal	adjective
resolve	noun, verb
principal	noun, adjective
access	noun, verb
label	noun, verb
phase	noun, verb

Exercise 3.2
a) noun
b) adjective
c) noun
d) verb
e) noun
f) verb
g) verb
h) verb
i) verb
j) adjective
k) adjective

Exercise 3.3
a) hypothesis
b) principal
c) access
d) stressed
e) phase
f) contrast
g) resolve
h) labelled
i) granted
j) internal
k) civil

Task 4
Exercise 4.1
Nouns: concentration, promotion, debate, statistics, investigation, occupation, option, access

Verbs: concentrate, promote, predict, investigate, occupy

Adjectives: subsequent, annual, debatable, predictable, occupational, optional, apparent, accessible

Adverbs: subsequently, annually, predictably, statistically, apparently

Exercise 4.2
a) investigation
b) statistics
c) predictable
d) accessible
e) concentrations
f) occupations
g) promotion
h) option
i) debatable
j) subsequent
k) Apparently

Exercise 4.3
a) debated; debate
b) access; accessible
c) occupied; occupation
d) predict; predictions
e) investigation; investigators
f) communication; communicators

Task 5
Exercise 5.1
a) inadequate
b) uncommunicative
c) recycle
d) unresolved
e) unpredictable

Exercise 5.2
a) recycle
b) adequate
c) unpredictable
d) unresolved
e) incommunicative

Task 6
Exercise 6.1
occupy France
grant permission
implement a strategy
implement recommendations
impose limits
impose a fine
give access
stress the need
carry out an investigation
have no option
have access
investigate the causes

Exercise 6.2

a) outcome; the future; the weather; rain; growth

b) independence; staff; control; heat

c) a crime; a robbery; an offence; suicide

d) the need; the importance; the urgency; the value

e) an action; an analysis; a project; a task

Exercise 6.3

a) retain; control

b) stress; importance

c) undertook; task

d) commit; crimes

e) predicting; growth

Exercise 6.4

prior notice

internal matter

inadequate provision

overall strategy

chief concern

Exercise 6.5

a) facts; evidence; problem; situation

b) impression; cost; majority

c) policy; wall; measurements; injury; inquiry; mail; trade; security

d) provisions; amount; funding; job

e) market; flight; appliance; life; violence

f) agreement; arrangement; engagement; warning; notice

g) defence; servant; law; liberty; order; authority; disobedience; engineering

h) case; question; situation

i) cause; issue; source; character

Exercise 6.6

a) need	**f)** commit
b) confirm, reject	**g)** break
c) show	**h)** have
d) make	**i)** have
e) require	**j)** achieve

Exercise 6.7

a) *official*	statistics
experimental	phase
high	concentration
a lot of; emotional	stress
economic; latest	predictions
high social	status
definite	goals

b) *According to*	statistics
of; with	stress
in	phase

c) integrated	*fully*
promote	*aggressively*
accessible	*easily*
communicate	*effectively*
contrast	*sharply*

Task 7

Exercise 7.1

• what prepositions are used to connect these nouns to following nouns

a) towards		**j)** to	
c) in		**k)** between	
d) of		**l)** to	
f) of		**q)** of	

• which nouns are followed by "*that* + clause"? (or *is/are* + *that* + clause)

b) attitude

e) prediction

r) hypothesis

• which highlighted noun is followed by a "preposition + *wh~* word + clause"

g) debate

• what preposition comes before contrast

l) in

• which nouns are followed by "to + infinitive"

h) job

i) commitment

• which highlighted word is not a noun, what word class it is and what comes after this word.

o) & p) despite, preposition, noun (the fact, treatment)

Exercise 7.2

life expectancy

distribution costs

prison sentence

weather conditions

research project

trade union

Exercise 7.3

a) human, computer, spelling

b) management, school

c) defence, survival, escape

Exercise 7.4

a) evident, significant, appropriate, positive, apparent, obvious, predictable
b) illegal, appropriate, abnormal
c) available, economical, traditional, valid, sufficient
d) use of *whether*

Exercise 7.5

a) passive
b) active
c) passive
d) active

Exercise 7.6

Transitive verbs: access, domesticate, internalise, implicate
Intransitive verbs: emerge

Exercise 7.7

Answers depend on dictionary used.

Exercise 7.8

Answers depend on dictionary used.

Exercise 7.9

a) VT   g) VI
b) VT   h) VT
c) VI   i) VI
d) VT   j) VI
e) VI   k) VT
f) VT   l) VT

Exercise 7.10

Answers depend on dictionary used.

Task 8

Exercise 8.1

a) prior notice
    subsequent side-effects
    difficult childhood
    criminal code
    principal cause
b) trade union
    transport strategy
    drug abuse
    school leaver
    identity card
c) stress
    investigation
    contrast
    commitment
    error

d) stress
    cycle
    contrast
    debate
    resolve

Unit 10: Academic Word List – Sublist 5

Task 1

Exercise 1.1

fundamental – the most essential and basic part of something
facilitate – to allow something to happen in an easier way
aware – to know of something's exsitence
symbol – a person or thing that is thought of as representing a bigger idea
modify – to make small changes to something to increase its effectiveness
challenge – something which tests a person's energy and determination
trend – a subtle change or development that seems likely to continue
substitute – something that is used instead of the one that you normally use, because the usual one is not available
enforce – to ensure someone abides by something
stability – the state of staying balanced and not altering
ratio – how two things relate to each other as numbers
transition – the change from one form or state to another
revenue – the monetary gain that a business organisation receives, often from sales

Exercise 1.2

a) revenue   h) enforced
b) aware   i) modified
c) substitute   j) facilitate
d) stability   k) symbols
e) welfare   l) transition
f) challenge   m) ratio
g) trend

Task 2

Exercise 2.1

1 c)   7 b)
2 a)   8 a)
3 a)   9 a)
4 b)   10 b)
5 b)   11 a)
6 a)

Task 3
Exercise 3.1

Word	Word class
prime	*noun, verb, adjective*
conflict	*noun, verb*
decline	*noun, verb*
challenge	*noun, verb*
contact	*noun, verb*
compound	*noun, verb, adjective*
monitor	*noun, verb*
network	*noun, verb*
reject	*noun, verb*
objective	*noun, adjective*
target	*noun, verb*
alternate	*verb, adjective*

Exercise 3.2
a) adjective   **g)** noun
b) noun   **h)** noun
c) verb   **i)** adjective
d) verb   **j)** verb
e) noun   **k)** adjective
f) adjective

Exercise 3.3
a) alternate   **g)** network
b) conflict   **h)** challenge
c) target   **i)** compound
d) declining   **j)** monitors
e) contact   **k)** prime
f) objective

Task 4
Exercise 4.1
Nouns: modification, symbol, substitution, rejection, precision, evolution, logic, consultation, expansion, adjustment
Verbs: modify, sustain, substitute, reject, evolve, consult, expand, adjust
Adjectives: symbolic, sustainable, stable
Adverbs: precisely, logically

Exercise 4.2
a) logically   **g)** evolved
b) stability   **h)** precision
c) alter   **i)** rejection
d) expansion   **j)** modifications
e) symbolic   **k)** sustain
f) adjustment

Exercise 4.3
a) adjust; adjustment
b) stability; stable
c) evolve; evolution
d) aware; awareness
e) consultation; consult
f) declining; decline
g) precise; precision

Task 5
Exercise 5.1
a) unaware   **e)** unmonitored
b) redraft   **f)** imprecise
c) illogical   **g)** instability
d) unsustainable

Exercise 5.2
a) aware   **d)** unsustainable
b) redraft   **e)** instability
c) monitored   **f)** imprecise

Task 6
Exercise 6.1
reduce stability
restrict access
make the transition
face a challenge
threaten targets
safeguard welfare
facilitate learning
exceed a limit
raise awareness

Exercise 6.2
a) challenge   **e)** reject
b) sustain   **f)** pursue
c) monitor   **g)** alter
d) generate

Exercise 6.3
a) pursued; policy
b) generated; jobs
c) monitor; progress
d) challenge; decision
e) pursue; ideas
f) generate; electricity

Exercise 6.4

present trends
rapid economic expansion
lost revenue
different versions
growing trend
prime cause
compound interest
greater awareness

Exercise 6.5

a) diet; country; marriage; building
b) affair; pressure; wall; examiner; use; source
c) issue; point; change; difference; error
d) example; candidate; time; Minister; factor; cost; target
e) conclusion; deduction; mind
f) work; fact; opinion
g) detail; cost; moment; nature; location

Exercise 6.6

a) transition — *make (the)*
    capacity — *work at; have (the)*

    image — *improve*
    conflict (with) — *come into*
    modifications — *make*
    its target — *reach*

b) adjustment — *slight*
    (at) ~ capacity — *reduced*
    perspective — *historical*
    version — *official*
    modifications — *minor*

c) evolved — *rapidly*
    aware — *environmentally*
    expand — *rapidly*
    monitor — *closely*

Task 7

Exercise 7.1

• what prepositions are used to connect the highlighted nouns to following nouns or gerunds

a) of   **l)** in
c) from   **m)** of
d) in   **n)** of
e) of   **o)** to
g) of   **p)** of
h) towards   **q)** about
j) with   **s)** for
k) of   **t)** of

• which highlighted noun is followed by
"*that* + clause"
f) notion

• which highlighted noun is followed by the verb
"*to be* + *that* + clause"
i) trend

• what prepositions come before *consultation* and *target*
j) *in* consultation
s) *on* target

• which highlighted noun is followed by
"*to* + infinitive"
b) capacity

Exercise 7.2

a) of   **d)** of
b) of   **e)** to
c) of   **f)** on

Exercise 7.3

air travel
blood flow
aviation fuel
exchange rate
heart disease
safety limit
freedom fighter
Internet access
sales target
interest rates

Exercise 7.4

a) sugar; teacher
b) level
c) media; television; radio; computer; train
d) book; vote

Exercise 7.5

• which adjectives are followed by "*to* + infinitive"
e) logical

• which adjectives are followed by "*that* + clause"
b) aware
g) logical

• which prepositions are used to connect the adjectives to following noun phrases
a) to   **f)** about
c) of   **h)** of
d) to

Exercise 7.6
Transitive verbs: compound, contact, enable, expose, liberalise, license, symbolise
Intransitive verbs: conflict

Exercise 7.7
Answers depend on dictionary used.

Exercise 7.8
Answers depend on dictionary used.

Exercise 7.9
a) VT
b) VI
c) VI
d) VT
e) VT
f) VI
g) VT
h) VI
i) VT
j) VI
k) VT
l) VT
m) VI

Task 8
Exercise 8.1
a) present trends
   fundamental change
   prime cause
   alternate weekends
   rapid expansion
b) exchange-rate stability
   tax revenue
   fossil fuel substitutes
   temperature monitor
   sales targets
c) consultation
   adjustment
   capacity
   symbol
   transition
d) compound
   decline
   challenge
   prime
   monitor

Achievement test answer key

Task 1
1 vary
2 restricted
3 dominant
4 apparent
5 aware

Task 2
1 c)
2 c)
3 b)
4 a)
5 c)

Task 3
1 verb
2 adjective
3 noun
4 noun
5 adjective

Task 4
Exercise 4.1
a) assessment
b) perception
c) implications
d) accessible
e) logically

Exercise 4.2
a) consultation; consult
b) declining; decline
c) precise; precision
d) stability; stable

Task 5
1 insignificant
2 unaffected
3 unreliable
4 recycle
5 imprecise

Task 6
1 evidence
2 impact / effect
3 coordinating / monitoring
4 hypothesis / theory
5 rapidly

Task 7
Exercise 7.1
a) preposition
b) preposition
c) preposition
d) *that* + clause
e) *to* + infinitive

Exercise 7.2
a) VI
b) VI
c) VT
d) VT
e) VT